Practising Gender Analysis in Education

Oxfam GB, founded in 1942, is a development, humanitarian, and campaigning agency dedicated to finding lasting solutions to poverty and suffering around the world. Oxfam believes that every human being is entitled to a life of dignity and opportunity, and it works with others worldwide to make this become a reality.

From its base in Oxford, UK, Oxfam GB publishes and distributes a wide range of books and other resource materials for development and relief workers, researchers, campaigners, schools and colleges, and the general public, as part of its programme of advocacy, education, and communications.

Oxfam GB is a member of Oxfam International, a confederation of 12 agencies of diverse cultures and languages which share a commitment to working for an end to injustice and poverty – both in long-term development work and at times of crisis.

For further information about Oxfam's publishing, and online ordering, visit www.oxfam.org.uk/publications

For further information about Oxfam's development, advocacy, and humanitarian relief work around the world, visit www.oxfam.org.uk

Practising Gender Analysis in Education

Fiona Leach

First published by Oxfam GB in 2003
© Oxfam GB 2003

ISBN 0 85598 493 7

A catalogue record for this publication is available from the British Library.

All rights reserved. Reproduction, copy, transmission, or translation of any part of this publication may be made only under the following conditions:
- with the prior written permission of the publisher; or
- with a licence from the Copyright Licensing Agency Ltd., 90 Tottenham Court Road, London W1P 9HE, UK, or from another national licensing agency; or
- for quotation in a review of the work; or
- under the terms set out below.

This publication is copyright, but may be reproduced by any method without fee for teaching purposes, but not for resale. Formal permission is required for all such uses, but normally will be granted immediately. For copying in any other circumstances, or for re-use in other publications, or for translation or adaptation, prior written permission must be obtained from the publisher, and a fee may be payable.

Available from:
Bournemouth English Book Centre, PO Box 1496, Parkstone, Dorset, BH12 3YD, UK
tel: +44 (0)1202 712933; fax: +44 (0)1202 712930; email: oxfam@bebc.co.uk

USA: Stylus Publishing LLC, PO Box 605, Herndon, VA 20172-0605, USA
tel: +1 (0)703 661 1581; fax: +1 (0)703 661 1547; email: styluspub@aol.com

For details of local agents and representatives in other countries, consult our website:
www.oxfam.org.uk/publications
or contact Oxfam Publishing, 274 Banbury Road, Oxford OX2 7DZ, UK
tel: +44 (0)1865 311 311; fax: +44 (0)1865 312 600; email: publish@oxfam.org.uk

Our website contains a fully searchable database of all our titles, and facilities for secure on-line ordering.

Published by Oxfam GB, 274 Banbury Road, Oxford OX2 7DZ, UK.

Printed by Information Press, Eynsham.

Oxfam GB is a registered charity, no. 202 918, and is a member of Oxfam International.

Photo acknowledgements
Front cover from left: Annie Bungeroth (East Timor and Pakistan); Sean Sprague (El Salvador)
Back cover: Ami Vitale (Senegal)

Contents

Acknowledgements vii
List of acronyms viii
1 Introduction 1
   Why we need gender analysis in education 4
   Gender debates 9
   Gender mainstreaming 12
   The role of gender analysis in achieving gender equality in education 13
2 Key concepts in gender and education 16
   Gender concepts 16
   Education concepts 23
3 Choosing your gender analysis tools 29
   Can these tools be used with men and boys? 34
4 The Harvard Framework 36
   Case study 1: a Nigerian teacher training college 41
   Case study 2: BRAC in Bangladesh 49
5 Women's Empowerment Framework 56
   Case study 1: the Tanzania Primary Education Project 60
   Case study 2: the *Reflect* programme in Ghana 66
6 The Gender Analysis Matrix 71
   Case study 1: a women's silk-reeling project in India 75
   Case study 2: the *Reflect* programme in Malawi 80
7 The Social Relations Approach 86
   Case study: HIV/AIDS education in Uganda 92
8 Curriculum-materials analysis 102
   Case study 1: a primary textbook from Malawi 114
   Case study 2: a primary reader for India 117
   Proposals for improvement 119

9 Participatory tools for analysis and action 124
   Limitations of the participatory approach 126
   Participatory tools 129
   Case study: pupils' workshop materials on abuse in African schools 142

Notes 150

Bibliography 152

Index 158

Acknowledgements

This book is intended as a companion to the earlier work *A Guide to Gender-Analysis Frameworks* by Candida March, Ines Smyth, and Maitrayee Mukhopadhyay and published by Oxfam in 1999. This in turn drew on a training pack prepared for Oxfam in 1996 by Candida March and supported by a number of Oxfam colleagues. Several of the frameworks selected here are also published in the 1995 *Oxfam Gender Training Manual*. This new book has similar aims to the earlier works, being broadly to develop awareness and skills in gender analysis, but this time with an education audience in mind. Inevitably, I have drawn heavily on the 1999 *Guide* and I am indebted to its authors for the assistance that this has given me.

I should like to thank ActionAid for allowing me to draw heavily on their *Reflect* materials, in particular the *Reflect Mother Manual* prepared by David Archer and Sara Cottingham and two *Reflect* evaluations. I also owe particular thanks to Sheila Aikman at Oxfam GB, who took forward the proposal for this companion to the earlier Guide to the publications board at Oxfam Publishing, and provided me with some case study material. I should also like to express my appreciation to Kate Newman and Kate Metcalfe at ActionAid, Annabelle Newbigging at DFID, and Marc Fiedrich (previously at ActionAid Uganda), and to my students from Nigeria and Bangladesh, for supplying some of the material used here. Also to Sara Cottingham, Sara Humphreys, Karen Hyde, Anna Obura, and Ines Smyth for commenting on earlier drafts, and to BRAC, DFID, and other organisations for permission to reproduce their material.

Fiona Leach
F.E.Leach@sussex.ac.uk

List of acronyms

ADEA   Association for the Development of Education in Africa
BRAC   Bangladesh Rural Advancement Committee
CBO   Community-based organisation
EFA   Education for All
GAD   Gender and Development
GAM   Gender Analysis Matrix
GER   Gross enrolment ratio
NER   Net enrolment ratio
NGO   Non-government organisation
PRA   Participatory rural appraisal
PRSP   Poverty Reduction Strategy Paper
SAP   Structural Adjustment Programme
SRA   Social Relations Approach
SWAp   Sector Wide Approach
UNGEI United Nations Girls' Education Initiative
UPE   Universal primary education
WID   Women in Development

1 | Introduction

Always ask: Where are the men? Where are the women? Why?
Gender Orientation on Development (1999), GOOD News, issue 11

This book

Practising Gender Analysis in Education is a companion volume to *A Guide to Gender-Analysis Frameworks* published by Oxfam GB in 1999. This latter book presented a number of analytical frameworks drawn from the Gender and Development (GAD) literature. I have been using a number of these frameworks in an educational setting for many years, both in teaching and research. As in other development contexts, they have helped to clarify issues of gender bias, discrimination, and inequality, and to identify possible strategies for addressing specific imbalances and injustices. However, it has been difficult to apply a framework designed for a development context, often with examples drawn from community-development projects, to an educational context. This book therefore draws on a number of the frameworks presented in the earlier book, suggests modifications to suit educational settings, and uses case studies drawn from education. In addition, I have widened the scope of the book to include a chapter exploring other appropriate tools of gender analysis, largely drawn from the Participatory Rural Appraisal (PRA) pool of resources, and also a chapter on curriculum-materials analysis.

Like the original volume, this is not a comprehensive manual of all the tools that can be applied to a gender audit of educational situations. It is a 'taster' of the many practical uses of such analytical tools. A full bibliography is provided at the end of the book.

This book makes a small contribution to ongoing efforts at gender mainstreaming in education by providing accessible tools for carrying out gender-sensitive analyses of current situations. These in turn should facilitate the planning of gender-sensitive interventions. Naila Kabeer (1996: 1), whose Social Relations Approach is outlined in chapter 7, points out that the major impetus for the design of analytical frameworks to integrate a gender perspective into the planning process has come from

a. the recognition that past policy interventions have been gender-unaware[1] and have resulted in avoidable costs and failures, and that new concepts and tools were needed to ensure greater sensitivity to gender issues;

b. the need to systematise and collate the insights of feminist scholarship and activism so that their relevance to the planning process would be more easily apparent to those not familiar with gender issues.

There are both efficiency and equity costs to gender-unaware policies where male norms supporting male preferences lead to a denial of access to capable women: the goals of development are thwarted and female autonomy eroded (*ibid*: 3–5). It is not that conscious decisions are taken to exclude or marginalise women from the planning process, but rather that there are 'unexamined assumptions and pre-conceptions which form the common sense of so much traditional top-down development planning'. At the same time, it is important to realise that some groups of men are also marginalised and disempowered in the planning process, and that gender analysis may need to take account of their needs while addressing those of women.

Gender mainstreaming is the internationally agreed strategy, adopted at the 1995 International Conference on Women in Beijing, for governments and development agencies to promote gender equality. In the education arena, the participating governments and agencies at the International Education Forum in Dakar in 2000 adopted a Framework for Action, which included among its six goals:

Eliminating gender disparities in primary and secondary education by 2005, and achieving gender equality in education by 2015, with a focus on ensuring girls' full and equal access to and achievement in basic education of good quality.
UNESCO 2002: 13

It also included the goal of achieving an improvement in levels of adult literacy by 2015, especially for women, and of ensuring that all children, including girls, children in difficult circumstances, and those belonging to ethnic minorities, are able to complete free and compulsory primary education of good quality.

These goals link up with two of the Millennium Development Goals agreed at the Millennium Summit of world heads of state in New York in 2000. These are (a) to achieve universal primary education and (b) to promote gender equality and empower women (*ibid.*).

This guide is intended for use by those working to achieve these targets in all types of educational settings: policy makers and planners, teachers and teacher trainers, academics, researchers and students, development agency staff, and other practitioners. It follows a similar format to the earlier book. Each chapter presents a tool for gender analysis and discusses its methodology and its uses as a means of supporting gender mainstreaming. It provides one or two practical examples of how the tool can be used, and draws out some of its strengths and disadvantages.

I use the term 'tools' here in a different manner to that used in *A Guide to Gender-Analysis Frameworks*. It is used here in a general sense to include the four gender analysis frameworks outlined (the Harvard Framework, the Women's Empowerment Approach, the Gender Analysis Matrix, and the Social Relations Approach), as well as the curriculum-materials frameworks and checklists in chapter 8 and the PRA activities and resources in chapter 9. A framework is understood here to be a self-contained and comprehensive model or method of gender analysis that one can apply to a particular context with the purpose of identifying key issues contributing to gender inequality. The other 'tools' are often small and uni-dimensional, and cannot generate a great deal of information on their own.

It is important to stress from the start that these tools should be used in a flexible way, and that expectations of what they can do for us need to be realistic. Nothing can replace more thorough forms of analysis, whether these are carried out through the collection and analysis of quantitative survey data (statistics), or qualitative research (descriptive findings from interviews, observations, etc.). They are, however, useful as a *starting point* for collective analysis and discussion and for the identification of strategies and action plans. Individuals and groups should assess the use for their own particular purpose of any of the tools described here. In the case of the detailed frameworks, it may not be necessary to go through the whole analysis as presented; alternatively, it may be necessary to modify it. However they are used, we do need to be aware of the risks of simplification and of assuming that there is some 'quick fix' offered by gender analysis. In all but the case of the Gender Analysis Matrix (GAM) detailed in chapter 6, these tools are only intended to provide a static snapshot at a particular moment in time. Their strength is in promoting understanding of gender inequality through *clarity* rather than through *complexity*. They help us to crystallise our thinking, isolate the important issues at key moments in time, and view the evidence in a stark light. The intention is to be analytical, rather than descriptive, and sensitive to diversity and context.

All the tools covered in this book can be used in ways which involve the target group(s) in some form of participation, very often in a workshop format, for example, as part of a gender training or awareness raising initiative. However, it is important to sound a note of caution about the power of participatory approaches (Fiedrich and Jellema 2003). We need to be aware that the potential for the 'feel-good' factor that participants in such workshops often experience can be misleading. These participatory activities can make people feel immediately empowered and resolved to take action to improve their circumstances, but they can also give an illusion of false consensus and false confidence. In the cold light of day their action plans, developed as part of a solidarity effort and requiring difficult changes in attitude and behaviour, may turn out to be too ambitious and remain unimplemented. Good intentions and enthusiasm can all too easily die away, and nothing changes.

Why we need gender analysis in education

Like its predecessor, this book is firmly grounded in the principles of social justice and respect for human rights. Gender equality is a priority for most development agencies, including Oxfam, in education as well as in social development. Denial of educational opportunity, like denial of access to healthcare, security, and opportunities for economic and social development, is a violation of human rights. Education plays a crucial role in teaching young people about their rights: their right to information, to services and political representation, their right to a 'voice' and to accountable government. No educational system should tolerate discrimination or inequality of any sort, as this is the very antithesis of 'education', its purpose being to release the potential in every human being. It is to be hoped that this book makes a small contribution to raising awareness of the importance of gender equality in education and offers some practical means of achieving it, as well as contributing to international efforts at gender mainstreaming.

Gender is, of course, not the only source of discrimination. Other markers of social identity are class, race, ethnicity, caste, sexuality, (dis)ability, age, and religion. It is important to recognise that these may interact with gender and where appropriate they need to be included in any gender analysis, as they affect women's and men's lives in different ways. The gender analysis tools presented here may in some cases be applicable to these other categories.

Universal primary education

Great efforts – and great gains – have been made over the past five decades to achieve universal primary education (UPE) and to make all citizens of the world fully literate. For many developing countries, the impetus came with political independence, mostly in the two decades following the end of the Second World War, as newly created national governments aspired to rapid economic development. Education as an investment in human capital was considered the key to this economic development; as the economy expanded, so would the demand for more skilled workers. Later, this view was revised to include education as an investment in social development, with clear links being made between education and health, low fertility and infant mortality, social welfare, and, more recently, democratic government, good governance, and respect for human rights.

Unfortunately, however, reaching the goal of UPE has been postponed time and time again; the latest declaration, at the Dakar Education Forum in 2000, has set a target date of 2015 for its achievement. In those countries yet to achieve UPE, there are usually unequal numbers of males and females who are denied access to education. According to the latest estimates (UNESCO 2002), of the 115.4m school-age children worldwide who are out of school, 56 per cent are girls. And of those adults who are illiterate, two-thirds are women (and it is roughly this same two-thirds who constitute the majority of the world's poor). There have been significant gains in access to schooling but these are uneven. In general terms, the better resourced the educational system, the higher the enrolments and the narrower the gender gap. So, for example, in Burkino Faso only 28 per cent of girls are enrolled in primary school compared with 41 per cent of boys; in Mozambique 46 per cent of girls compared with 55 per cent of boys; and in Gambia 65 per cent of girls compared with 75 per cent of boys. This can be compared with a situation where there is a much smaller gap, for example, in Thailand, where 80 per cent of girls are enrolled and 83 per cent of boys; in Indonesia 90 per cent of girls are enrolled and 93 per cent of boys; and in Costa Rica 91.1 per cent of girls and 91.4 per cent of boys (*ibid.*). On the whole, girls drop out of education in greater numbers than boys where overall survival rates are low and gender disparities high. In some countries with high enrolments, however, an opposite picture emerges, with more girls enrolled and staying on in school than boys, for example, in most Caribbean and South American countries, Philippines, Thailand, Sri Lanka, and some Southern African countries such as Namibia, Lesotho, and Zambia. In many of these countries, too, national data show that girls' achievement is also higher than that of boys. There is increasing evidence of boys playing truant and dropping out of school, even in the less well-resourced countries where national data still show them achieving better examination grades than girls. So the picture is complex, and boys too are at risk.

Education For All

In the early days of rapid expansion of schooling, the problem of access to education for children was seen as just a matter of building more schools to expand the number of available places and recruiting and training more teachers. Non-physical barriers, whether economic, social, political, or cultural, were not, on the whole, understood. Remarkably, it was not until 1990, when an international conference on Education For All (EFA) was held in Jomtien, Thailand, that the international community fully realised that UPE could never be achieved until the issue of girls' under-representation in education was addressed. One of the most urgent priorities for the decade-long EFA initiative became, therefore, the improvement of educational opportunities for women and girls (WCEFA Final Report 1990). This has led to a shift away from an exclusive preoccupation with resourcing education to a concern for equity in education.

Halfway through the decade, however, statistics showed that despite this focus on girls' education, their share of primary education had only increased by less than half a per cent, and that 73m girls still remained out of school (Leach 2000a). In some regions (parts of Sub-Saharan Africa and South and East Asia), the gap between boys' and girls' enrolments was, in fact, rising. At the start of the twenty-first century, it remains the case that, despite some gains, in the poorest countries of Sub-Saharan Africa, South Asia, and in the Middle East, fewer girls enroll in school, they tend to drop out in larger numbers than boys, and they have lower achievement. They make up the majority of children out of school in the world. In rural or isolated areas of these countries, literacy levels among women can be extremely low, for example, only 15 per cent among rural women in Bangladesh (BRAC 1998), less than ten per cent in remote parts of Afghanistan and Pakistan.

Lack of access, or limited access, to education has a negative impact on young people's life opportunities, their ability to earn a living, to fulfill career aspirations, to enjoy a productive life, and to exercise autonomy and choice if they so wish. Demographic changes have come about as a result of the decline of the extended family, the increase in divorce and female-headed households, and the impact of the HIV/AIDS epidemic, in particular the vulnerability of women to infection. Increased poverty has also led to a growth in child labour and human trafficking. It is therefore essential that every person can take full opportunity of whatever educational provision there is, however limited. Although girls and women are disproportionately disadvantaged globally, there are also boys and men who are exploited, impoverished, and marginalised. Education is crucial for them too.

So, why has progress been so poor? Why, despite all the public commitments and policy statements since 1990 by donors, lenders, and governments on the need to increase female participation in education, and so many programmes directed specifically at getting more girls into school, has progress been so slow? This can be in large part explained by a narrow focus on girls that does not consider the gendered nature of the society in which schools operate. This is culturally sensitive ground, embedded with a multitude of traditions, norms, and values relating to gender roles and relations, and to status and power in what remain heavily patriarchal social systems. Perceptions about the value of educating girls as well as boys and about appropriate roles for girls and boys when they reach adulthood, the availability of jobs, the needs and interests of the household, and also the attitudes and aspirations of girls themselves, all act as barriers to girls' educational opportunity. Schools themselves play a major part in reinforcing these gendered views, and so just getting more girls into school does not guarantee equality of opportunity or outcome. Unfortunately, the drive for gender equality is largely made by the international donor agenda. This creates situations of weak compliance by governments committed on paper to the EFA goals and, not surprisingly, results in what is called 'policy evaporation'. This is where the commitment to pursue equality remains at the level of rhetoric and paper statements, and is not integrated into the actual design and implementation of reforms.

The new discourse of equity and inclusion within development agencies and national governments fits badly with the dominant economic imperative behind much educational policy. So, the introduction of structural adjustment programmes (SAPs) in many of the poorer countries during the 1980s has led to the imposition of school fees, increasing privatisation, and an expectation that communities will contribute to the building and running of schools. These are all likely to undermine efforts to get girls into school, as the education of boys is, on the whole, given priority over that of girls, and to reduce the chances of the goal of EFA being met within the set time frame. This economics-driven agenda conflicts with the social development agenda around human rights, equity, and justice.

At the same time, even in countries where girls stay on in education in greater numbers and achieve better results in exams, this is not necessarily reflected in their subsequent participation in the labour market and in political life. Women are still paid less than men, even in the most industrialised countries, and they are disproportionately to be found in unskilled or semi-skilled jobs, and on the margins of economic activity, for example, in petty trading and occupations that are casual, unstable, labour intensive, and vulnerable to exploitation. The latest figures provided by the Human Development Report (UNDP 2002) show that the highest ratio of female to male share of national income is to be found in Finland, where for every US$ 100 earned by males on average, a female only earns $70, while in the UK the female average is $61, and in Italy and Japan a mere $44. In Canada, women make up 35 per cent of female legislators, senior officials, and managers (the highest figure globally), but in Australia the figure is only 26 per cent, in Italy 19 per cent, and in Korea a mere five per cent. Women are also very poorly represented in the political arena globally, whether as Members of Parliament or in high-ranking government appointments. In the UK only 18 per cent of MPs are women, in Canada 24 per cent, in the USA only 14 per cent, in Japan ten per cent, and in Italy nine per cent. Clearly there are still barriers that prevent women from fulfilling their potential in employment and in the public arena as well as in education.[2] This suggests the need to examine the gender ideology that still prevails in the family, in state institutions such as schools, and in the labour market.

There has been a great deal of educational research in the developed world around gender issues in schools, and the role of the school in socialising adolescent girls and boys to accept adult roles and patterns of behaviour which comply with dominant social norms, including expectations of appropriate female and male occupations. This research has almost exclusively focused on the ways in which schooling has disadvantaged girls, although there has been some research focused on socio-economically disadvantaged boys. Research in schools in developing countries is very limited, but studies from the English speaking industrialised countries (for example, UK, USA, Australia, and New Zealand) have uncovered a range of influences which appear to have a negative impact on girls' participation and achievement in schooling, and so also on their career choices. These include

- teaching styles which favour boys, such as lessons which focus on memorising abstract facts, as opposed to open-ended, process-oriented tasks, which girls favour;
- boys' dominance in classroom interaction, which marginalises girls' participation;
- subject-choice, with girls opting or being encouraged to opt for 'feminine' subjects such as languages, history, and literature, while boys go for the so-called 'hard' subjects of maths, science, and technology, especially as these are seen to lead to careers and better paid jobs;
- assessment styles which, according to some research, favour boys, such as multiple-choice questions, whereas girls are known to excel at course work;
- marker bias, which gives boys' work higher marks;
- teachers' lower expectations of girls;
- girls' own lower self-esteem and self-confidence;
- teachers' own attitudes to gender values which, despite many believing that they treat girls and boys equally in the classroom, suggest that girls are 'passive' and boys are 'boisterous' (as summed up in the saying 'boys will be boys').

However, since the early 1990s in the developed world, the school performance of girls has caught up with that of boys, and in many countries boys now lag significantly behind girls, (for example, in much of Europe, the USA, and Japan). An adverse male peer culture, which promotes a dominant view of masculinity that is anti-school and anti-authority is seen as very much to blame.

So the picture is complex. To fully understand why there are these continuing disparities in educational opportunity, we need to engage in gender analysis of all aspects of educational provision, whether these are policies, institutions, curricula, teaching approaches, or forms of assessment.

This can help us to understand why girls in some situations drop out of school, why boys in others are becoming increasingly disaffected and prefer to play truant, and why the literacy or training that disadvantaged adult women and men acquire does not empower them by allowing them to make informed choices or to earn a decent living.

Gender debates

The WID/GAD debate

There is a traditional distinction drawn between the Women in Development (WID) approach and the Gender and Development (GAD) approach. WID was very much a feature of the late 1970s. It was the 1975 International Conference on Women in Nairobi, pushed by the feminist movement in the industrialised world, which turned global attention towards the position of women in the developing world. This led to the establishment of women's organisations, ministries of women, women's units or bureaux within existing ministries, and policies in governments and development agencies to promote the integration of women into the development process. The focus was on promoting the productive role of women, that is, their contribution to economic development, which had been largely ignored at that time. Not surprisingly, women's income-generation projects were popular.

Disillusionment with the WID approach emerged in the early 1980s, when little progress had been made in improving the condition of women. The realisation that WID had changed nothing, that women remained marginalised and silenced, and that women's projects were not part of the mainstream of development shifted attention to the gender dimension of development. We realised that we cannot expect dramatic change if women are treated as passive beneficiaries of development interventions, and efforts are made to tackle their short-term problems without addressing the inequalities that are embedded within gender relations. We need to look at why women are marginalised, not just in what way. We need to understand the underlying causes of their under-representation, not just the outward appearance. This thinking was influenced by feminist activism: women need to be agents of change, to organise themselves to take control of their lives.

By the mid 1990s, WID had become GAD in most development agendas; however, there was a great deal of confusion, with many projects and programmes containing the word 'gender' in their title but in reality still espousing a WID approach. Two main strands of GAD emerged: the efficiency approach and the empowerment approach. In the efficiency approach, attempts were made to incorporate gender analysis in the planning of all development interventions through an enhanced understanding of men's and women's roles and responsibilities, to ensure greater effectiveness by including women in economic development (the Harvard Framework presented in chapter 4 follows this approach). In contrast, the empowerment approach built on the interest in participatory methods of engaging in development. It focused on the empowerment of women through increasing their awareness of the gendered structures and power relations within which they operate, their self-confidence and their participation in the development process (the Longwe Framework presented in chapter 5 fits with this). Both approaches, however, have tended to focus on 'what women could do for development rather than on what development could do for women' (Derbyshire 2002: 9).

The efficiency approach remains the dominant adaptation of WID since the 1980s and the approach most favoured by the World Bank and many development agencies (despite their use of the equity discourse). Their argument is that economies are inefficient if they do not harness the full potential of half their population and restrict them to domestic and reproductive roles. Women's participation in the labour market is therefore strongly encouraged.

Table 1.1, from Annabelle Newbigging's gender guidelines for DFID education advisors, effectively illustrates the way in which thinking on WID and GAD has developed over the past three decades.

Men and masculinities

Recent interest surrounding men and masculinities in development raises questions about how gender can be made an issue for men as well as for women, without marginalising women in the process (Chant and Gutmann 2000: 4). This has, over the past decade or so, become a familiar question for development agencies: how to empower women without antagonising men? Increasingly, we also have to ask: how to assist the growing numbers of men who are also poor, oppressed, and vulnerable? The commonly held assumption that men are oppressors and women are victims is a simplification of reality, and not helpful in addressing either male or female gender needs in a lasting manner. As Andrea Cornwall (2000: 24) points out, we need to view gender not as a unilateral women's issue but in terms of relations of power and powerlessness in which men as well as women may be vulnerable and disempowered. We need to find constructive ways of working with men to transform power and gender relations without marginalising women. There is little evidence, however, of male-inclusive gender and development initiatives to date, and there remains considerable concern that 'bringing men in' will undermine the hard work already done to advance women's interests.

As explained above, boys now under-perform relative to girls in many educational contexts, including some parts of the developing world. This has led to an interest (in the UK, for example) in looking at the ways in which the school culture helps to construct particular versions of femininity and masculinity among pupils. In this, the peer group is seen as reflecting these

Table 1.1 Changing approaches to women's issues

The Welfare Approach (1970s)	Addressed women's needs in the context of their roles as wives and mothers, i.e. projects focused on childcare and domestic tasks. *Critique:* this was felt to perpetuate inequality, as men gained exclusive access to new technologies and women were left behind.	women as a target group
Women in Development Approach (WID) (mid 70s– mid 80s)	Aimed to integrate women into economic development. Established WID projects and departments and income-generation projects for women. Feminism persuaded women to be 'agents of change'. Distinction between 'sex' and 'gender' arose. *Critique:* there was a failure to look at how and why women were disadvantaged. Many income-generation projects failed.	
Gender 'efficiency' and 'empowerment' approaches (late 80s– mid 90s)	'Efficiency' approach: gender analysis (i.e. understanding women's and men's roles and resources) makes good economic sense. 'Empowerment' approach: working with women at the community level, building self-esteem and determining needs. *Critique*: mixed success on both approaches. Issue of policy evaporation and of development organisations themselves being part of the problem.	gender equality as a goal
Gender mainstreaming approach (mid 90s, post-Beijing)	Attempts to combine strengths of efficiency and empowerment approaches. Involves ensuring that women's and men's concerns are integral to the design, implementation, monitoring, and evaluation of all legislation, policies, and programmes. This also concerns staffing, procedures, and culture of development organisations and is the responsibility of all staff.	▼

Source: Newbigging 2002a: 11

prevailing versions of female and male identity. Peer group cultures play a central role in determining what young people come to define as 'success' in the school context, especially for secondary-age pupils (Arnot *et al.* 1998: 73). This process is influenced by ethnicity and social class as well as by gender. For boys, this has resulted in a range of different masculine identities. Among low-achieving boys from a low social class, this peer group culture often results in an anti-school attitude, challenging adult authority, truancy, and homophobia (Willis 1977, Mac an Ghaill 1996). As traditional forms of employment for young males in Western Europe such as mining and heavy industry have disappeared, and women's views of marriage and careers have changed, adolescent males have developed 'cultures of resistance', which include resistance to schooling. In such a peer culture, many boys are victims of bullying and exclusion from the group if they do not conform to dominant masculine behaviours. The view that boys are at risk in school is relatively recent, but we need to bear this in mind when engaging in gender analysis.

The gender analysis tools outlined in this book can all be applied to men and boys (even the Women's Empowerment Approach). They already look at gender roles and relations, with this one exception, and so could be applied to projects targeting men and/or boys as well as to projects that seek to assist both sexes. Our dilemma is really the extent to which the analysis, as with projects and programmes, seeks to raise issues of gender so as to improve women's and girls' autonomy and quality of life, or whether it should address both, in so doing risking a dilution of efforts at helping women and girls. There is increasing evidence that not all men regard social expectations of what it is to be male (bravery, virility, wise decision making, the ability to earn a living and provide for a family) as desirable (Castells 1997, Cornwall 1998). To male adolescents, these expectations can be frightening, a burden from which they cannot escape. At school, too, the construction of opposing female and male identities is in many ways destructive of potential on both sides.

Gender mainstreaming

Attempts to combine both the efficiency and the empowerment approaches have led to what is called 'gender mainstreaming', already referred to above. Annabelle Newbigging describes this as

> ... a commitment to ensure that all women's as well as men's concerns and experiences are integral to the design, implementation, monitoring and evaluation of all legislation, policies and programmes so that women and men benefit equally and inequality is not perpetuated ... Gender mainstreaming is integral to all development decisions and interventions; it concerns the staffing, procedures and culture of development organisations as well as their programmes; and it forms part of the responsibility of all staff.

Newbigging 2002a: 9

Gender analysis provides a crucial element of that strategy, and gender analysis frameworks a powerful tool for doing it.

Over the past few decades, the impact of projects and programmes seeking specifically to address women's issues has often been disappointing because they focused only on gaining access for women to the benefits of these interventions. They may have had some impact on the re-distribution of resources controlled by the project or programme but did little to change social perceptions of gender and the nature of dominant gender relations. Hence the current interest in gender mainstreaming. This does not exclude women-only projects, but shifts the focus from women as a target group to gender equality as a goal. Gender mainstreaming can support both women-only and men-only projects as strategic interventions to address gender inequalities.

Different approaches to mainstreaming exist. These are outlined in *A Guide to Gender-Analysis Frameworks* (p.10). On the one side, mainstreaming is seen as the responsibility of everyone in the organisation, so that gender concerns are integrated into all structures and all activities. On the other, this is seen as diluting the issue so that gender risks disappearing altogether through lack of commitment, leadership, and focus; advocates on this side argue for small specialist teams or units dedicated to the task of ensuring that gender issues are given high visibility and addressed at all levels. Yet a third approach has been to establish national 'machineries' or specialist teams (ministries, women's bureaux, etc.) but these have tended to be under-resourced and ignored when important policy decisions need to be made. What is disturbing is that although gender and women's issues are increasingly included as a category in discussions and plans, all too often this is tokenism. The consensus at present seems to be that organisations need to engage in both the integration of gender concerns throughout the organisation and the use of specialist departments or units so as to avoid marginalisation and co-optation of gender issues.

The role of gender analysis in achieving gender equality in education

It is crucial that participants at all levels of the current international efforts to achieve good quality Education For All understand the importance of addressing the gender aspects of their efforts. By learning to engage in rigorous gender analysis, using both quantitative and qualitative indicators, we can better understand the level of gender disparities in educational provision and identify appropriate strategies to address them. Gathering sex-disaggregated statistics is essential for this purpose. However, qualitative data is also necessary, so that we can appreciate the complex causes and consequences of such disparities.

The new integrated approach to development assistance adopted by the World Bank and others during the 1990s has at times threatened to swamp equity goals, including gender goals. The move away from funding discrete projects to an enthusiastic embrace of sector-wide approaches (known as SWAps) to aid coordination means that there is a need for concerted advocacy efforts to ensure that gender equality goals are incorporated at the macro-level in sector-wide policies and plans. So far, compliance is weak. SWAps require development partners to work to a common agenda, and it is expected that this agenda will be owned and led by local stakeholders in an inclusive approach embracing government, lenders and donors, and civil society organisations. However, in aiming for an integrated approach, it is easy for pressing economic issues such as securing resources to take precedence over longer-term and seemingly intractable gender issues. This is especially the case where men dominate the policy discourse – efficiency is likely to take precedence over equity (Terry 2001).

In the same way, gender risks being sidelined by the World Bank and IMF's new Poverty Reduction Strategy mechanism, which is intended to help the most heavily indebted countries to obtain debt reduction. A Poverty Reduction Strategy Paper (PRSP) covers all sectors of development including education. Despite global initiatives such as the UN Girls' Education Initiative (UNGEI), which was launched after the Dakar 2000 World Education Forum as a partnership of 13 UN organisations to help governments to meet their commitments on girls' education, and the Global Campaign for Education, foregrounding gender issues in national policy frameworks remains a considerable challenge. It is depressing that, despite explicit commitments to prioritise gender in Jomtien in 1990, reiterated in Dakar in 2000, so few education policy documents provide evidence of serious engagement with gender issues. The Tanzanian primary education policy document, which provides the context within which the Oxfam project detailed in chapter 5 was intended to operate, is one example of a recent national policy statement which makes only passing mention of gender and contains no sex-disaggregated data.

Annabelle Newbigging (2002b), in her survey of gender training and awareness raising activity among 14 donor agencies, found evidence suggesting that the policies and programmes which demonstrate the greatest success in working towards gender equity goals are informed by gender analysis, and incorporate specific action to promote gender equality. Action is most effective when backed up by human and financial resources and monitored with sex-disaggregated indicators. Gender awareness is required at every stage of the programme cycle. This requires gender training of staff, but not in the form of one-off gender-sensitisation courses or workshops that only pay lip-service to the need to address gender issues. Training needs to be embedded in the specific context being addressed, and needs to be ongoing.

Newbigging also found that the majority of interviewees expressed a need for gender 'tools' tailored for the education sector, to help advisers address gender issues. Some agencies have developed these, but others felt that more is needed. 'We have general instruments for gender mainstreaming, but nothing specifically for the education sector ... We feel it is important to combine a mixture of general gender concepts as well as focusing on practical tools' (ibid.: 8–9). It is here that gender-analysis frameworks can help to move forward gender mainstreaming work, as they facilitate an understanding of the gender power relations and inequalities that exist in any particular institutional environment, such as the school, the workplace, or the family. This is essential if advocacy work on gender is to be effective. This book is designed to make a contribution to addressing this need.

Further reading

Chant, S. and M. Gutmann (2000) *Mainstreaming Men into Gender and Development: Debates, Reflections, and Experiences*, Oxford: Oxfam GB.

Fiedrich, M. and A. Jellema (2003) *Literacy, Gender and Social Agency: Adventures in Empowerment*, London: DFID.

Jayaweera, S. (1997) 'Women, education and empowerment in Asia', *Gender and Education*, 9(4): 411–23.

Leach, F. (2000a) 'Gender implications of development policies on education and training', *International Journal of Educational Development*, 20(3): 333–47.

Newbigging, A. (2002a) 'How can Education Advisors help to achieve the PSA Gender Equality Targets: Guidance sheets for promoting equal benefits for females and males in the Education Sector', London: DFID (Education Department).

Global Coalition for Education (2003) 'A Fair Chance: Attaining Gender Equality in Basic Education by 2005', Global Campaign for Education, available from www.campaignforeducation.org

2 | Key concepts in gender and education

Introduction

To use the gender analysis tools effectively, it is essential to have a clear understanding of the central concepts being used. That is not to say that their meaning is necessarily straightforward and uncontested. Some, including the meaning of the term 'gender' itself, are the subject of debate and disagreement. They are explained here in broad terms, however, starting with gender concepts and then moving to educational concepts.

Gender concepts

Sex and gender

These terms are not interchangeable. One is biologically determined and the other socially determined. Sex is an easier term to define than gender, being the biological difference between men and women. Only women can give birth and only men can produce sperm.[3] By contrast, gender is a culturally relative term derived from the social sciences; it is the product not of biology but of social practice. Understandings of gender, and the 'practice' of gender, differ widely between societies (and also between members of a particular society); this may lead to very different experiences of what it is to be male or female. Gender is used to describe all the socially driven aspects of our lives: the roles we play, the responsibilities we take on, our expectations for the future, and the behaviour and activities we engage in. There are strongly held views about what is considered appropriate female and male behaviour in different societies. Concepts of gender are dynamic and change over time. Our gender identity is formed during our early years and largely determines how we perceive the social world and how we are perceived by others. School experiences are a crucial part of this identity formation, and schools and other educational organisations are as marked by gendered practice as any other institution.

Sex stereotyping/bias

Extreme cases of negative sex stereotyping can be found in common sayings such as the following (from UNESCO's 1997 *Manual on Gender Sensitivity*): 'Women in the field damage the crop' (Bangladesh); 'Behind a loser stands a woman' (Philippines); 'A hundred sons are not a burden but one daughter bows our heads' (Pakistan); and 'Without a man, the family is a house without a roof' (Vietnam). More universal comments about a woman's place being in the home, about women being poor or erratic drivers, or as being emotional or illogical, are so frequent that they are easily absorbed into our subconscious, reinforcing a negative 'deficit' image of women. Textbooks and other teaching and learning materials are a prime source of sex stereotyping (see chapter 8).

Gender relations

This refers to social interaction and social relationships between women and men, both in the private and the public arena. Gender relations can involve cooperation or conflict, trust or suspicion, partnership or competition, love or hate, tenderness or violence, and complex combinations among them. Gender relations are influenced by other markers of social identity such as class, race, ethnicity, religion, and age. Increasingly, social science research intersects gender with other social categories, for example, gender and race in the classroom, gender and class in the workplace. Fundamental to gender relations is the concept of power and its unequal distribution. Gender identity and gender relations are performed differently in different contexts and they may change over time. This can be seen in the way in which the social and economic roles of women have become much less restrictive in many countries, largely as a result of economic development and industrialisation. This has created job opportunities for women and given them unprecedented levels of economic independence. The feminist movement has also been powerful in changing gender relations and perceptions of appropriate roles for women, with more women now being seen in visible public positions, for example, as Members of Parliament and government ministers. Schools have certainly served to widen girls' horizons in particular, and co-educational schools have the opportunity to foster constructive interaction and mutual understanding between the sexes from an early age. At the same time, highly defined gender relations between female and male pupils, between female and male teachers, and also between teachers and pupils (and in some cases between head teachers and teachers), continue to be a prominent feature of all co-educational schools. This is not surprising, because to a large extent schools reflect norms of behaviour which exist in the wider society.

Gender roles

These are patterns of behaviour that assign specific tasks, responsibilities, and obligations to men and women. Gender roles are determined by social and economic factors and by the norms and values that underpin what we do. As such, they are also dynamic and subject to change. They help to determine the amount of power and status accorded to individuals. Some tasks are mistakenly claimed to be determined by sex (biology), such as child rearing or earning family income, but in fact they are determined by social views of what is appropriate. Men can be just as good at raising children as women, and women can be just as competent breadwinners as men.

The tasks carried out within these gender roles are often categorised as 'productive' and 'reproductive'. This is referred to as the 'sexual division of labour' but, as these tasks are largely socially determined, the term 'gender division of labour' would be more accurate. In each society, certain tasks are deemed suitable for men and others for women; sometimes there is no clear distinction. In most societies, the tasks associated with males usually have higher status and value than those associated with females. This usually allows men to exercise more power. The school is not immune from these influences, and studies show that even in schools with female head teachers, male teachers are likely to wield more power and are given a greater role in decision making than female teachers (Dunne, Leach *et al.* 2003).

Productive and reproductive work

Productive work refers to activities carried out to provide goods and services for income or subsistence. Both women and men carry out productive work but it is not valued equally. Productive work in the formal economy, such as a waged or salaried job, and sometimes self-employment, is included in national economic statistics, whereas much productive work in the informal sector is not included. Women work disproportionately in the informal sector in small-scale activities, and this work is less visible and less valued.

Reproductive work refers to all the tasks involved in the care and maintenance of the household and its members, including child bearing and child rearing, cooking, cleaning, and caring for the sick. This work is not usually paid, is often not seen as 'real work', and is not valued as much as productive work. It is not counted in national economic statistics. It is labour intensive and is overwhelmingly carried out by women and girls. There is likely to be a social stigma attached to men carrying out this work.

From a recent study in junior secondary schools in Botswana and Ghana (Dunne, Leach *et al.* 2003), it was found that female pupils carried out tasks associated with female domestic roles, such as sweeping classrooms and offices and fetching water, while boys did weeding, gardening, cleaning windows, and carrying heavy loads. Boys were rarely found with brooms or mops and were more often supervising girls' tasks than doing them themselves. Likewise, outside classroom teaching teachers, carried out tasks traditionally associated with their gender: male teachers were associated with tasks involving public events or physical exercise such as organising sports days and school trips, or supervising work in the school grounds, while female teachers busied themselves with hospitality for visitors, fetching the tea during staff meetings, and counselling pupils.

The study also found that quite young pupils had very clear ideas of which tasks are suitable for boys and which for girls; they even tended to conscientiously 'police' the gendered allocation of duties themselves, claiming that the strict segregation of duties was to avoid ridicule; boys as well as girls would laugh at a boy who did sweeping, for example.

Triple role

Caroline Moser (1993) has suggested a third category of work – *community work* – and so she has coined the term 'triple role' to describe women's work. Community work involves contributions to what is known as civil society (NGOs, community associations, religious groups, women's groups, campaign networks, parents' associations, and so on), as well as the collective organisation of social events, such as wedding and funeral ceremonies and services in the community. This work can be divided into two types: community management (provision and management of community resources such as water, healthcare and education, and social events), which is largely voluntary and unpaid, and community politics (local lobbying groups and local politics, community representation at higher levels of government, etc.), which may be paid for. Again, the former is largely carried out by women, the latter largely by men. The latter usually carries a higher social value.

In the Tanzanian project used as a case study in chapter 5, it is interesting to note that women contributed most to the school in monetary terms and attended parents' meetings, but were poorly represented on village and school committees.

Gender analysis

This involves examining relationships between women and men, and the inequalities and power differences between them, in a systematic way. When engaging in gender analysis, we have to ask questions such as: Who does what? Who owns what? Who makes decisions? Why is it like this? Gender analysis may need to intersect with other social indicators such as class, race, age, or religion, as experiences of gender are likely to differ greatly depending on whether you are middle class or working class, white or black, Hindu or Moslem, young or old. Within these categories, too, there will be a wide range of experiences. Gender analysis may also cut across the home, the community, the State and the labour market, and may be carried out at local, national, and international levels. The aim of gender analysis is to unpack the hierarchical nature of gender relations as part of a broader social analysis, to determine what changes are required if more equitable relationships are to result, and ultimately to promote a more equal society.

Sex-disaggregated data

This is information collected separately about men and women (or male and female children), so that it is possible to examine different trends, patterns, and levels of participation, in schooling or in types of employment, for example, and so seek the underlying causes for the differences observed in the data. Such data are essential in identifying strategies to increase school enrolments or to provide effective adult education. Some governments still do not gather sex-disaggregated data on school enrolments, or do not release it to international organisations such as UNESCO.

Gender needs

The concept of gender needs, as being either *practical* or *strategic*, is widely recognised by those working within the field of gender and development. The original concept was developed by Molyneux (1985) and then taken up by Moser (1993) in her book *Gender Planning and Development*, where she incorporates it into her gender-planning framework. Gender needs vary widely according to socio-economic context, and according to race, class, and other social categories. They are primarily seen as women's needs within an unequal relationship with men. However, men also have gender needs: for example in terms of such issues as childcare, paternity rights, and military conscription. Both sexes have gender needs regarding sexual orientation. A focus on gender needs should not ignore the fact that women, men, and children all have *rights*. Topics on human rights, democracy, and citizenship are increasingly appearing in school curricula worldwide, but the reality of many school environments is one of authoritarian management, a didactic teaching style, and excessive corporal punishment, which gives no space to the exercise of children's rights at all.

Caroline Moser defines *practical gender needs* as 'the needs women identify in their socially accepted roles in society. Practical gender needs do not challenge the gender divisions of labour or women's subordinate position in society, although rising out of them. Practical gender needs are a response to immediate perceived necessity, identified within a specific context' (1993: 40). Immediate perceived necessity might be shelter, work, credit, healthcare, or education, for example, which would be addressed by providing specific inputs such as health clinics or schools.

Moser defines *strategic gender needs* as 'the needs women identify because of their subordinate position to men in their society. Strategic gender needs vary according to particular contexts. They relate to gender divisions of labour, power and control and may include such issues as legal rights, domestic violence, equal wages and women's control over their bodies' (*ibid.*: 39). They can only be realised when women's subordinate position is challenged, and changes brought about to the existing roles, legal entitlements, and institutional practices which impact on gender relations. The goal of the feminist movement has been the realisation of women's strategic gender needs.

Strategic needs can be addressed through practical needs. Sara Longwe (1998) points out that every practical development intervention has an effect on power relations and so impacts on strategic needs. Her Women's Empowerment Framework suggests a movement from practical needs (welfare and access) to strategic needs (conscientisation, participation, and control) but this may not necessarily be in a linear manner. The distinction between practical and strategic needs in the real world may also not be clear-cut, for example, access to contraception is a practical need but it can (and has) resulted in wide-ranging strategic gains for women. Education, of course, addresses practical needs (ability to read and write, knowledge of health and hygiene) but it should also address strategic needs in terms of providing young people with greater life choices in terms of careers, marriage, informed decision making, and so on.

Gender equality versus gender equity

These terms are often used interchangeably but equality in fact refers to the concept of equal rights and entitlements, equity to fairness and justice. Gender equality refers to the norms, values, and attitudes that allow for equal status between women and men without ignoring biological differences. Gender equity refers to fairness in women's and men's access to resources. It does not mean that everyone should be treated the same, or that it is necessary to have equal numbers of women and men in any institution or profession. Derbyshire (2002: 7) distinguishes between equality of opportunity (equal rights and entitlements to human, social, economic, and cultural development, and an equal voice in civic and political life) and equity of outcomes (the exercise of these rights which leads to fair and just outcomes). In some cases, equality of opportunity is seen to require affirmative action if imbalances in equality of outcome are to be addressed. To encourage more female teachers in Bangladesh, for example, there has been since 2000 a policy to recruit only female primary teachers on government salaries, and the entry requirement to teacher training is also lower for women than for men (secondary school certificate for women, higher secondary school certificate for men).

Empowerment

This is a slippery and much over-used term. At the most basic level, it refers to the process or processes whereby people become aware of their own interests and the power dynamics that constrain them, and are then able to develop the capacity and the means to take greater control of their lives (without infringing the rights of others). It builds on the Brazilian educator, Paolo Freire's concept of *conscientisation* (Freire 1970), that is, developing a critical understanding of one's circumstances and social environment that will lead to action.

People need to become aware of their own interests, both as individuals and as a group, and to see themselves as able and entitled to make decisions (Rowlands 1999). However, there is a great deal of rhetoric around notions of power, empowerment, and participation, as the extract from Fiedrich and Jellema (2003) in chapter 9 makes clear.

Gender-blind (or 'gender-unaware')

Policies, plans, programmes, or individuals may not recognise that gender is an essential feature of life choices and of power relations. So, if they tend to favour male views or priorities, they will exclude women without being conscious of it. Gender is not an issue. Gender-unaware policies and plans may be couched in apparently gender-neutral language but they are implicitly male-biased in that they privilege male needs, interests, and priorities in the distribution of opportunities and resources. Chapter 8 will provide examples of ways in which the school curriculum is often gender-unaware, in particular in terms of the use of subject matter, illustrations, and language in textbooks.

Gender-neutral

Policies, programmes, plans, and curriculum materials may be labelled 'gender-neutral'. This means that they recognise the existing gender division of resources and responsibilities, and seek to ensure that objectives are met as effectively as possible without seeking to alter these divisions. They do not seek to change gender relations, therefore, but rather to work within the current differences in society, that is, they may pursue practical gender needs but not strategic ones. In the context of development aid to education, the revision of textbooks and curriculum materials has been a popular target for funding. This has often resulted in materials that are gender-neutral rather than gender-unaware. For example, the Malawi textbook used for analysis in chapter 8 is an improvement on its predecessor (the revision was funded by a number of donor agencies) but is still not immune from gender stereotypes.

Gender-sensitive

This means that policies, programmes, and plans do in fact identify gender relations as problematic and offer opportunities for an examination and discussion of gender issues. They deal with strategic as well as practical issues. As far as teaching and learning materials are concerned, a gender-neutral approach would involve trying to omit all portrayal of men and women in stereotypical roles, avoiding reference to 'he' or 'his' as a generic term, and having an equal balance of images of males and females. A gender-sensitive approach would specifically address gender issues so as to destroy stereotypes and present a new way of perceiving men, women, and their relationships.

Many schools are gender-unaware places, where neither teachers nor pupils perceive gender as being an issue that needs to be addressed.

Gendered school practices such as giving separate tasks to female and male pupils are seen as 'natural', and bullying and other forms of aggressive behaviour, largely from boys, as 'part of growing up'. However, there are teachers who make a conscious effort to use the subject matter of lessons to engage pupils in a gender debate and to provide opportunities for discussions around topics such as the family, equal opportunities, and women's liberation. Many schools have a commitment to gender equality as one of their aims but do little to see it turned into reality.

Gender budgets

This is a new area of gender analysis. As Derbyshire (2002: 18) explains: 'Gender budgets ... are analyses of government budgets to establish the differential impact of revenue raising or expenditure on women and men and on different groups of women or men. They are designed to inform public policy debate, and as such are a particularly important lobbying tool in the context of national policy frameworks'. Budgets are usually gender-unaware and, unless they are analysed using sex-disaggregated data and other gender-sensitive information, it cannot be known how much of a particular budget is having an impact on women and how much on men. A gender budgeting exercise can look at either expenditure or revenue and can be carried out by organisations such as government bodies, NGOs, and schools. The most common approach to gender budgeting is as part of a policy appraisal. It assumes that budgets reflect policy. Newbigging (2002a: 24) provides an Indian case study of a gender-budget analysis in the education sector.

Education concepts

Formal, non-formal, and informal

This book provides examples of both formal and non-formal education programmes. *Formal* education refers to the national, standardised system of education that leads to certification and qualification, for example, school, college, and university. *Non-formal* education refers to organised learning outside this framework, which does not usually lead to national qualifications (although some may provide certificates). Leisure courses for adults, vocational training, and literacy classes are usually classified as non-formal education. Almost all the educational programmes offered to adult women, out of school children, and adolescent drop-outs are of the non-formal type. Most NGOs focus on non-formal education. In this book, the case studies are drawn from a range of contexts: formal education (schooling), non-formal education (adult literacy), formal training (of teachers) and non-formal training (business skills). *Informal* education is unplanned learning that takes place throughout our lives. It occurs when we are interacting in our families or with friends, watching TV, a film, a sports event, etc.; it also occurs in formal and non-formal educational settings, but outside the framework of the planned learning event such as a lesson or lecture. Traditionally, the extended family and the community pass on livelihood skills, cultural heritage, sex education, etc. to children. Humans engage in social interaction and in this process much learning takes place. Sometimes, more is learned informally at school than formally.

Basic education

This refers to the basic (usually compulsory) cycle of formal education. In the better-resourced educational systems, this usually means 11 years of formal education (age five or six to age 16 or 17 is the most common). In the poorer countries, primary schooling may constitute the basic cycle, in others primary and junior secondary (eight or nine years in all). In some countries, junior secondary is supposed to be compulsory but some parents cannot afford to pay fees and so do not send their children; alternatively, there are insufficient places for all children in the age group. In others, entry to junior secondary is by competitive exam at the end of primary. Basic education is supposed to include non-formal education, but most development agencies concentrate on formal education only. Non-formal education is grossly under-funded and neglected.

Reasons why girls participate less in the basic cycle of schooling than boys in many of the poorer countries are often identified as 'barriers'. They include:

- lack of school places;
- distance to school;
- costs of schooling (fees, uniforms, books, etc.);
- the need for girls to perform domestic duties at home;
- early marriage;
- and parental views of the lower value of educating girls.

Evidence for girls' (or boys') lower participation has to be based on gender-sensitive data, such as:

- the ratio of boys to girls in school and out of school;
- levels of truancy, absenteeism, and drop-out among both girls and boys;
- and differential achievement levels in national examinations.

Education for All (EFA)

In 1990, a World Declaration on Education For All was adopted at the World Education Conference in Jomtien, Thailand. This was an international commitment to provide access to good quality education for all citizens, as well as to address the diverse learning needs of children, youth, and adults. This vision of a basic education for all could be realised both through formal and non-formal education programmes. In Dakar in 2000, the World Education Forum re-affirmed this vision, and adopted a Framework for Action that emphasised the need for quality in basic education as well as access to it. Six goals were agreed on at Dakar, all of which have gender implications. As already noted, two of these Dakar goals are also Millennium Development Goals (UNESCO 2002) and they are supposed to link up to PRSPs and SWAps and other international and regional initiatives. A major international effort is currently underway to see these goals realised by 2015.

Universal Primary Education (UPE)

Over the past four decades, there have been many international targets to get every school-age child into school, starting from 1960. The target date has always been deferred, so that it now stands at 2015.

Dissatisfaction with the exclusive focus of development efforts on primary schooling to the neglect of non-formal modes of learning and post-primary schooling, (which in better-resourced systems is part of the compulsory cycle, that is, junior secondary), led to a broadening of the range of internationally funded initiatives at the Jomtien 1990 World Conference on Education for All. They now encompass what is known as 'basic education'.

Curriculum v. syllabus

A syllabus usually refers to the programme of learning for a particular subject for a given period, one school year, for example. By contrast, the curriculum refers to the full range of subjects offered in a school or other educational institution. So, for example, in a particular country there may be eight compulsory subjects on the junior secondary curriculum, plus a number of optional subjects (of which the pupil may be required to pick one or two). Each subject will have its own syllabus for each year of study. Extra-curricular activities refer to activities carried out at school but outside the context of the formal lessons, for example, in clubs such as sports, dance, chess, or photography, or in school choirs and orchestras.

Supply and demand

Educational systems in most developing countries have focused on supply – to provide enough school places for all school age children. Less focus has been paid to demand, as it has always been assumed that demand will remain until universal access is achieved. Increasingly, however, there is evidence that not all parents believe in the value of schooling. Many poor parents prefer to keep their children at home to look after younger siblings or to work on the land, in the marketplace, or in waged labour. The poor quality of teaching and learning, poor facilities, high absenteeism among teachers, sexual harassment and abuse by some male teachers and pupils, the misappropriation of school funds, and other issues have reduced the demand for schooling, in particular of girls.

Access and retention or survival

Most national education statistics distinguish between access to education (initial enrolment at the start of the compulsory cycle) and retention or survival (those who complete each cycle). In the least-resourced systems, many students drop out after two or three years of schooling. The number completing the primary or basic education cycle may be only a fraction of those who entered. Poverty, low demand for education (especially for girls), and poor quality of the learning environment are all factors that contribute to irregular attendance and drop-out.

Achievement

This refers to pass rates in examinations. In most African and South Asian countries, national data show that girls under-achieve relative to boys, while in most of the developed world and the Latin America and Caribbean regions, the opposite is the case. However, within any one country there may be considerable disparity in achievement rates, for example, between private and public schools, urban and rural schools, well-resourced and less well-resourced schools, and between social and ethnic groups.

Structural adjustment programmes (SAPs) and PRSPs

Initiated in the 1980s, SAPs were financial policy guidelines required by the World Bank and the IMF before the poorest countries could qualify for grants or loans. They tended to centre on a number of key areas of macro-economic policy such as liberalisation, deregulation, decentralisation, and privatisation. They led in most countries to the introduction of school fees during the late 1980s and 1990s, usually at the secondary level but sometimes also at the primary level. It is widely claimed that the marked deterioration of basic services such as health and education in the poorest countries is the direct result of the stringent requirements of SAPs (Rose 1995, Stromquist 1997). SAPs were seen not to have been effective in reducing poverty, and on the contrary, often led to increased debt without addressing structural barriers to development. They are now being replaced by PRSPs (Poverty Reduction Strategy Papers) (Terry 2001).

Education indicators

The most common indicator used in national and international statistics is enrolment (number of pupils who enroll in the first year of schooling, number of learners who enroll in a literacy class, etc.). A gross enrolment ratio (GER) is the most common statistical measurement, as it is the easiest to collect: it refers to the number of pupils enrolled in a given level of education regardless of age, expressed as a percentage of the population in the relevant official age group. The GER may be higher than 100 per cent as a result of grade repetition and entry at younger and older ages than the typical grade-level age. In contrast, the net enrolment ratio (NER) refers to the number of pupils within the official age bracket for a given level who are enrolled in that level (e.g. 6–11 for primary, 12–16 for secondary), expressed as a percentage of the total population in that age group; this provides a more reliable picture of the proportion of the school-age population in school. Survival rates (those who complete the full cycle), repetition rates (those who repeat a class), attendance (those who actually turn up to classes) and achievement or attainment (those who pass national exams, usually at the end of the cycle) in fact provide a much more reliable picture of what is going on. Unless separate figures are gathered for males and females on all these indicators, it is impossible to monitor the extent to which the gender gap in education is closing.

Human capital

Education is considered as an investment in human capital. Human capital is usually defined as the body of knowledge, skills, and competencies embodied in individuals that contributes to a country's economic activity. Human capital theory claims that improving the educational level of a nation's workforce leads to increased productivity and hence to economic growth; education is therefore an investment in future economic prosperity. The focus on economic growth meant that most efforts at educational expansion for many developing countries in the early years of independence were directed at the education of males as future members of the workforce.

Social capital

Recently there has been a shift of interest in the international community away from a preoccupation with human capital as the basis for economic growth towards an examination of the role that social capital plays in social and economic development. The concept of social capital is contested, but Bourdieu defines it as 'the product of investment strategies, individual or collective, consciously or unconsciously, aimed at establishing or reproducing social relations that are directly useable in the short or long term' (Bourdieu 1986: 249). Social capital can be seen either as an element of class formation based on the elitist and inherited nature of social networks, or as membership of community and social networks which contribute to collective well-being. According to the latter view, communities that have high levels of social capital and social cohesion experience a better quality of life than communities with low levels. In the context of schooling, there is an increased awareness of the social benefits of education and attempts to teach social and life skills (including health education) and concepts of democracy and citizenship to young children, so that they can create high levels of social capital as adults.

Further reading

Freire, P. (1970) *Pedagogy of the Oppressed*, New York, NY: Continuum.

Longwe, S. (1998) 'Education for women's empowerment or schooling for women's insubordination?', *Gender and Development*, 6(2): 19–26.

Molyneux, M. (1985) 'Mobilization without emancipation? Women's interests, state and revolution', *Feminist Studies* 11(2).

Moser, C. (1993) *Gender Planning and Development: Theory, Practice and Training*, London: Routledge.

Rose, P. (1995) 'Female education and adjustment programs: a cross-country statistical analysis', *World Development*, 23(11): 1931–49.

Rowlands, J. (1999) 'Empowerment examined', in *Development with Women: A Development in Practice Reader*, pp. 141–50 (first published in *Development in Practice*, 1995, 5(2)).

Stromquist, N.P. (1997) 'Gender sensitive educational strategies and their implementation', *International Journal of Educational Development*, 17(2): 205–14.

UNESCO (2002) *Education for All: Is the World on Track?* EFA Global Monitoring Report, Paris: UNESCO.

UNESCO (1997) *Gender Sensitivity: a Training Manual*, Literacy Section, Basic Education Division, Paris: UNESCO.

See also www.reflect-action.org for further discussion of participation and empowerment.

3 | Choosing your gender analysis tools

Introduction

The gender analysis tools presented in this book are designed for flexible use so that they can be applied to many different contexts and purposes. They can be used at all levels and stages: for policy formulation and budgetary analysis; planning both small and large scale educational change; project or programme design, implementation, and evaluation. Annabelle Newbigging (2002a: 14) illustrates this well (see Figure 1).

The gender analysis tools can also be used in research studies and advocacy work. They are effective because they crystallise the issues in an easily accessible manner. In this respect, they are a valuable assistant in the promotion of gender mainstreaming.

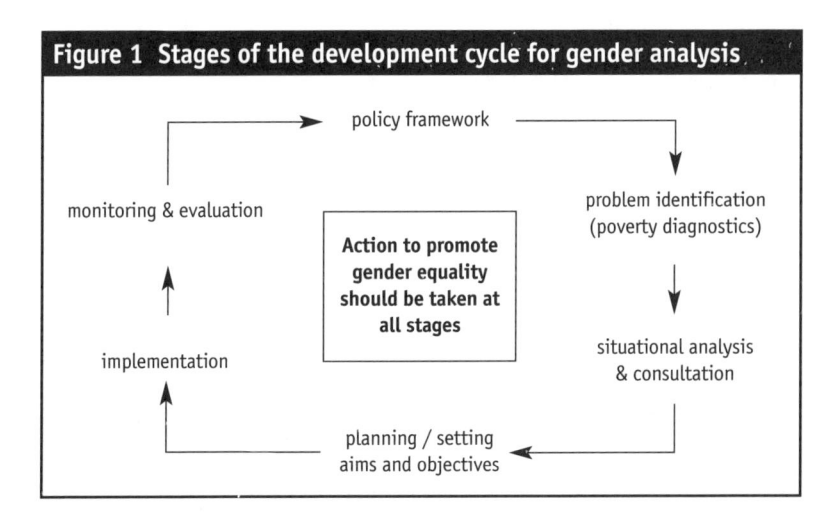

Figure 1 Stages of the development cycle for gender analysis

policy framework → problem identification (poverty diagnostics) → situational analysis & consultation → planning / setting aims and objectives → implementation → monitoring & evaluation → (back to policy framework)

Action to promote gender equality should be taken at all stages

The broad aim of all the tools presented here, whether termed 'framework' or 'approach' or 'activity', is to facilitate the analysis of gender issues in educational contexts, and the planning of appropriate interventions to promote greater gender equality in educational settings. Analysis and action plans go hand in hand. These tools encourage clarity of thinking; they help you to work through the issues that contribute to gender inequality in a particular situation, and to start to identify ways in which they can be addressed. They allow you to get to the heart of the problem by separating out the essential features of the situation from the superfluous detail.

The four gender analysis frameworks included here share some common concepts about gender: for example, that women have multiple roles (reproductive, productive, community maintenance) and needs that are both practical and strategic. They also share the assumption that women are generally more disadvantaged than men, and so the frameworks are used mostly to address women's needs. As already stated, they can be applied to other settings where some form of inequality, disadvantage, or marginalisation occurs, such as ethnic minorities, disabled people, or certain groups of men. The analysis can also be multi-dimensional, cross-cutting gender with other indicators of social inequality. These frameworks are useful tools in the face of complex social realities, where they can help to draw attention to the key issues that have to be addressed if we are to achieve certain goals.

In using the tools presented in this book, it is not necessary to engage in extensive analysis. However, the more superficial an analytical exercise, the greater the risk of a distorted reality. There is also the risk of over-generalising, seeing groups as uniform rather than made up of diverse individuals, so that they are identified only according to broad categories of common characteristics, for example, poor, ethnic minority, women, illiterate.

It is also important to realise that the power of these tools is limited; we need to be realistic about what can be achieved. They are only a mechanism for analysis, they do not lead automatically to action or to an improved set of conditions. They are imprecise tools that present a crude model of reality. With this in mind, these tools should not be used on their own if they are part of a formal project or programme. They need to be included as part of a well-defined process of needs assessment, evaluation, development of viable strategies, and so on, which may involve a range of other sources of evidence such as documentary material, interviews, and surveys. They are also not neutral. The choice of tool, how it is used, the particular issues identified that are followed up all depend on the perspectives, assumptions, and values of those who use them.

These tools are practical instruments, designed to help you to integrate a gender analysis into on-going development work. They assume that the situation of women (and men) to which they are being applied is unsatisfactory and needs to be changed. They can be combined and/or modified to suit particular purposes. In this book they have been adapted to an educational setting and their use is illustrated by case studies drawn from a range of educational contexts. The fundamental aim in whatever context they are used, however, is to address issues of gender inequality in an accessible way.

Choosing your gender analysis tools

In choosing which of the four frameworks to use in a particular context, you need to take into account the designer's own values and assumptions regarding gender, as this will influence the type of analysis you engage in, which in turn will influence the type of action that is recommended to address the particular gender inequality under scrutiny. So, you need to consider what aspects are appropriate in your work, and what purpose you are trying to achieve, when making your choice. As the authors of the 1999 *Guide to Gender-Analysis Frameworks* have pointed out, the frameworks have been designed for very different purposes. They summarise these diverse purposes as:

Context analysis: these tools give you a way of thinking about the context that shapes the relationships and dynamics of any situation or group.

Visualisation and planning: the tools provide you with a way of representing key points in a simple manner, to aid decision making.

Communication: the tools help you to share information, train people, or sensitise them to gender issues.

Monitoring and evaluation: the tools can highlight the strengths and weaknesses of a particular development intervention.
(March *et al.* 1999: 27)

Your choice of framework needs to take into account the two contrasting views of why we should address gender inequality, which were presented in chapter 1: the *efficiency* argument and the *empowerment* argument. It is important to be aware of the thinking that underlies each framework before making a choice of which one to use.

Efficiency

The efficiency approach to women in development is based on the understanding that it is inefficient to ignore women in development initiatives. It aims to create projects and programmes with the most efficient allocation of resources, which may mean allocating resources for different purposes and in different amounts between women and men. Although this approach seems very sensible, there are times when it can come into conflict with wider issues of justice or women's empowerment. As a consequence, the efficiency approach has been heavily criticised because it has failed to challenge existing gender relations and so has tended to lead to gender-neutral or gender-specific policies or interventions. Because resources, not power, are seen as central, it can also further tip the balance of power in the favour of men if a decision is taken to allocate more resources to men on the grounds of efficiency. This could be detrimental to women. Similarly, if it does not make a project more efficient to involve women, then following the logic of the efficiency argument you should not do so.

This approach can be particularly problematic in countries where women are not well-educated and not usually involved in production outside the home. In education, this would be problematic where, for example, a government policy included the aim of a balanced representation of women and men in key decision-making positions in the Ministry of Education, but where there were very few women in middle ranking or senior positions who can be promoted. Promoting a more junior person with limited experience might jeopardise the chances of educational policies and plans being implemented. Likewise, selecting an equal number of men and women for an advisory team, or as head teachers, or for training purposes might not be efficient if experienced men are left out. So, equity criteria are often in conflict with efficiency criteria.

The **Harvard Framework** is most clearly located within this efficiency argument. Because of its emphasis on the allocation of resources and activities, it lends itself particularly well to organisational analysis. This is illustrated by the Nigerian case study in chapter 4, where the framework becomes a powerful tool for identifying inequitable allocations of roles and responsibilities. However, it can also be applied to policies, projects, programmes, sectors, and sub-sectors, as is illustrated by the second case study, which makes a broad comparison between BRAC schools and government primary schools in Bangladesh.

The **Gender Analysis Matrix** also takes into account efficiency considerations, as it suggests an analysis based on categories such as labour, time, and resources. It allows you to measure changes to these categories over time as part of a project or programme intervention. This is its main strength; the other frameworks do not lend themselves so well to measurements over time. It differs from the Harvard Framework in that it is rather unwieldy for organisational analysis. Rather, it gives an excellent view of how situations involving women, men, children, and communities change as a result of a particular input such as skills training or literacy. It is used here to monitor changes on a project that provided training in small-business skills to women, and another using the *Reflect* literacy programme in Malawi.

Empowerment

Other frameworks have the explicit aim of empowerment. These emphasise the transformation of gender relations through providing women with the enabling resources that will allow them to take greater control of their lives.

This is self-empowerment, a process which may not meet efficiency criteria at all, as it is a long and risky undertaking, which the disadvantaged group must itself initiate and sustain.

The **Women's Empowerment Framework** (Longwe) is the obvious example of this approach. It is a very versatile and simple framework, which can be applied to most situations. It is designed to measure the extent to which women have been empowered through gaining access to, participation in, and control of the development process. It lends itself better to the analysis of projects and programmes than to organisational analysis. It is particularly effective at measuring the extent to which women (and men) participate and control projects and programmes. It could also be used to analyse very specific aspects of projects and programmes, such as gender budgeting. The framework is illustrated here by a study of an Oxfam-supported primary education project in Tanzania and a *Reflect* literacy programme in Ghana.

Although the **Gender Analysis Matrix** (GAM) can be used to measure efficiency gains, it can also measure empowerment. The author suggests a category of analysis entitled 'cultural factors' which allows you to measure the impact of the intervention on women's and men's social status (in the case study illustrated in chapter 6, the researchers chose to call this 'social impact').

The **Social Relations Approach** (Kabeer) also allows for an analysis of gender relations in terms of empowerment. Its strength over the other frameworks is that it allows you to carry out an inter-institutional analysis, for example looking at how to design an intervention that takes into account gender relations within the family, the labour market, the community, and the State. None of the other frameworks makes this an easy option. As its name suggests, its focus is on gender relations as a form of social relations, rather than on roles or resources. It allows for a close analysis of the way in which different forces help to shape and to constrain social relations. It is a more wide-reaching and comprehensive tool, and in some ways more challenging. It can, however, be used in a simpler way to analyse a single institution or organisation. It is used here to examine reasons why schools have had only a limited role in HIV/AIDS prevention programmes in Uganda. It does this by drawing on all four institutions suggested by Kabeer (with education as representative of the State) to show how these forces interact at different levels of the household, the labour market, the community and the State to weaken the impact of health messages in schools.

All these frameworks can be used in a participatory mode; however, some lend themselves more readily to this than others. The GAM and the Women's Empowerment Approach both make a participatory approach central to their methodology. However, they do not need to be. PRA tools must, by their definition, be used in a participatory mode but what counts as 'participatory' is also open to interpretation, as we have heard from Fiedrich and Jellema (2003).

In all of the above, the concepts of practical and strategic gender needs and of women's triple role (productive, reproductive, and community) are useful dimensions.

The tools for **curriculum materials analysis** are specific to teaching and learning materials, but these can be of a widely varying type (non-formal as well as formal, basic literacy materials as well as textbooks used at university level, newspaper articles as well as novels). They can also be applied to the texts of magazines, plays, video or televised material, and collections of drawings or photographs, and to school prospectuses and publicity materials. They vary in the categories of analysis adopted by each, and their level of detail. For example, the UNESCO training manual on gender sensitivity provides a straightforward checklist, whereas the Obura and FAWE frameworks cover both quantitative and qualitative analysis in great detail. FAWE's *ABC of Gender Analysis* allows for an analysis of the text in the classroom context, not just on the written page.

Participatory tools for analysis and action: these draw on the PRA (Participatory Rural Appraisal) approach to community development, and are intended to be used in a workshop format. They are effective in stimulating discussion around community issues, identifying problems, and seeking action among those who usually lack a 'voice' in local and national affairs. Specific activities need to be created to meet the desired objectives of the workshop and should take into account whether the participants are children or adults, mixed or single-sex groups. A trained facilitator should always be used. Examples are provided from a research study investigating the abuse of girls in African schools.

Can these tools be used with men and boys?

Gender analysis frameworks have not usually been used to identify male issues to be addressed through action. The gender dimension has revolved around analysing the relationships between women and men, so as to see how best to meet women's needs. However, over the past decade there has been a growing awareness that identifying and addressing gender issues does not necessarily mean a focus on women's issues only. Men can also be disadvantaged, marginalised, and oppressed. Poor men, for example, refugees, migrant workers, unemployed or disabled men, men from ethnic or religious minorities, as well as men who do not conform to dominant views of masculinity such as homosexual men or pacifists in time of war, may be as vulnerable to discrimination and as exposed to violence as women. There is also increasing awareness that gender identity interacts with other forms of social identity and so a gender analysis needs to be multi-dimensional. A gender project therefore needs to include men's needs and interests as well as women's (even the perceived needs of powerful men, if only to help plan more effective gender-sensitive or gender-redistributive[4] policies). The same applies to the school context: there is increasing evidence that strategies to address the range of gender disparities that impact disproportionately on girls (including gender violence in school), will only be successful if both female and male pupils and teachers are involved in seeking solutions.

Of the gender analysis frameworks included in this book, the **Harvard Framework** specifically looks at women's needs (practical and strategic), but an adaptation of it by the Development Policy Unit (DPU), University College London, which is included in an appendix to *A Guide to Gender-Analysis Frameworks*, includes men as well and so can be used to address men's needs and projects. Sara Longwe's **Women's Empowerment Framework** only addresses women's needs, but there is no reason why it should not be used to cover both. The **Gender Analysis Matrix** does examine the impact of the change on men's activities, status, etc. alongside women's (children, household, community may be other categories) and can easily address both women's and men's needs.

Explaining the chapters

Each of the following chapters provides a description of a particular gender framework or tool and suggestions as to how it can be modified for application to an educational (or training) setting. Four of the gender frameworks found in the volume by March *et al.* (1999) are illustrated here within an educational or training context. These are supplemented by chapters covering the use of participatory tools for gender analysis in education and tools for the analysis of curriculum materials.

Each chapter starts with a brief introduction explaining the origin of the framework or tool, and outlining its basic principles. The reader is then shown how it can be applied to an educational context, with suggested modifications, and this is illustrated through one or two case studies. There is then a commentary on its practical uses and its limitations, and its strengths and weaknesses. Each chapter ends with a set of useful references. These are also included in the bibliography at the end of the book.

The case studies are taken from a range of formal and non-formal contexts: schooling, teacher training, adult literacy, and training for women (in this instance in business skills). All are broadly educational in that they exemplify planned teaching and learning encounters in an institutional context, although as is customary those with fixed outcomes in terms of specific skills to be acquired are usually labelled 'training'.

4 | The Harvard Framework

Introduction

The Harvard Framework was one of the earliest attempts to apply gender analysis in a structured way to development activities. It was developed at the Harvard Institute for International Development in the USA, working in collaboration with the WID office at USAID. It is fully explained in Overholt *et al.* (1985) *Gender Roles in Development Projects*. This framework belongs to the earliest phase of interest in gender, which concentrated on increasing the recognition of women's role in economic development by focusing on efficiency considerations. Not surprisingly, therefore, it emphasises women's productive role.

Basic principles

The focus of the framework is on access to and control of resources, emphasising the importance of economic considerations in working towards gender equity. It allows planners and development workers to map the range of **activities** engaged in by men and women, to assess their respective **access and control** of the resources needed for these activities, and to identify **influencing factors**. There is also a **project cycle analysis**, consisting of a checklist of questions to use when assessing proposals or interventions in terms of their sensitivity to gender issues.

The framework should be used as a starting point for a detailed analysis of the ways in which the formulation and interpretation of policy, the design of a project or programme, or daily organisational practices (both formal and informal) can lead to and reinforce gender discrimination and stereotyping. The four components of the framework are the activity profile, the access and control profile, the set of influencing factors, and the project cycle analysis. Although the opportunity to modify the categories of analysis is important, it should be remembered that the framework can never capture the full complexity of the circumstances to which it is applied; it merely helps to clarify the differentiated impacts and implications for women and men and girls and boys.

In the following sections, the Harvard framework is presented first with the original categories from Overholt et al.,[5] and then with two examples of how it can be adapted, the first looking at an activity profile and an access and control profile of staff and students in a teachers' college, the second at an access and control profile of staff in BRAC schools in Bangladesh as contrasted with those in government schools.

Activity profile

In its original form, the Harvard Framework identified activities as either productive or reproductive. As explained in chapter 2, Caroline Moser (1993) later added a third category: community activity. She divided this into community management (largely female) and community politics (largely male). Subsequently, the term 'triple role' for women became common.

Completing the matrix shown in Table 4.1 allows for the identification of all relevant productive, reproductive, and community tasks carried out by women and men separately, and answers the question: Who does what? The categories 'men' and 'women' can be broken down into male child, female child, or into further sub-categories based on ethnicity, age, or class, for example, or by location, such as home, school, or community. The first case study below modifies these categories to suit the context being analysed (college, home, and community) but other categories may be appropriate, for example, relevant categorisations in a school setting may be formal and informal roles of teachers or pupils, or classroom and other (extra-curricular) roles of teachers, or management and teaching staff roles.

Table 4.1 Activity Profile

	Women / girls	Men / Boys
Productive		
Reproductive		
Community		

Adapted from March et al. 1999: 33

Table 4.2 Access and Control Profile

	Access		Control	
	Men	Women	Men	Women
Resources				
Land				
Equipment				
Labour				
Production				
Reproduction				
Capital				
Education / training				
Benefits				
Outside income				
Assets ownership				
In-kind goods (food, clothing, shelter, etc.)				
Education				
Political power / prestige				
Other				

Source: Overholt 1985:12

Access and control profile

The access and control profile is divided into two categories: resources and benefits. It allows for the detailed listing of the resources available to men and women, and identifies who has access to them, who controls them, and who controls the benefits that arise from their use. This is a helpful distinction because all too often projects have focused only on ensuring access for women or marginalised groups, and have ignored the issue of who controls them (and the subsequent outputs).

Table 4.3 Influencing factors

Influencing factors	Constraints	Opportunities
Community norms, cultural beliefs, economic factors, organisational practices, etc.	Lack of mobility, early marriage, poverty, lack of political will, etc.	Government priorities, lobbying by women's groups, externally funded projects, etc.

Adapted from March *et al.* 1999: 35

Influencing factors

This allows for the identification of factors which influence who has access to and control of resources.

By identifying constraints, we are better able to look for opportunities which will facilitate a more equal sharing of resources and more involvement in development projects, and perhaps in this way increase income and well-being. An example of this in an educational context is provided in Table 4.8.

The concept of practical and strategic gender needs can easily be mapped onto the above profiles, as is done in Table 4.4 with the activity profile.

Table 4.4 Activity profile and gender needs

Roles	Women	Men	Gender needs met	Gender needs met
Productive				
Reproductive				
Community				

Project cycle analysis

This consists of a series of questions designed to help examine a project proposal or intervention using sex-disaggregated data and capturing the different effects of social change on men and women. The full version is not provided here but is available in its original form in Overholt et al. (1985) and in *A Guide to Gender-Analysis Frameworks* (pp. 36–8).

In an educational context, this may be of use with projects designed to improve some aspect of the educational system, for example, to increase the number of female head teachers in schools, or to increase community involvement in local schools (and ways in which women's involvement can be assured).

Table 4.5 Key topics for questions on project intentions
Women's dimension in project identification
Assessing women's needs
Defining general project objectives
Identifying possible negative effects
Women's dimension in project design
Project impact on women's activities
Project impact on women's access and control
Women's dimension in project implementation
Personnel
Organisational structures
Operations and logistics
Finances
Flexibility
Women's dimension in project evaluation
Data requirements
Data collection and analysis

Source: Overholt *et al.* 1985: 13–15

Applications to educational settings

The Harvard Framework can be modified to facilitate the gender analysis of structures and practices within educational organisations. As the following case study from Nigeria shows, it can reveal discrimination and stereotyping which exists either in formally sanctioned procedures or in routine daily practices. Both limit access and control of resources (including decision making) by different groups. It is therefore a tool that contributes to gender mainstreaming and to supporting equal opportunities and staff-development policies.

Application of the Harvard Framework to an organisational setting allows for a deeper understanding of the gendered nature of the organisation than can be revealed by basic statistics. It can, if done in collaboration with staff, lead to awareness raising, discussion of the causes and consequences of the under-representation of women, and possible changes in policy or practice.

The first case study is an analysis of a teacher training college in Nigeria. It uses an activity profile (examining the division of roles and responsibilities of both staff and students in the college), an access and control profile (for staff only), and a chart detailing the factors which are likely to have contributed to differentiated staff activity and access and control, together with the constraints and opportunities for change. It has been compiled with information gathered for a Ph.D. thesis. Although not included as part of the original research design, the researcher has used it to clarify key concepts and uses.

The second case study is taken from the BRAC Non Formal Education Programme (NFPE) in Bangladesh, with an access and control profile for teachers in BRAC NFPE schools being compared with that of teachers in the government school system. The same comparison could be done for pupils. This comparative dimension provides an illuminating analysis of the extent to which BRAC does in fact provide a girl-friendly environment compared with government schools. The actual categories chosen for the analysis are dependent on a group's (or team's) particular aims for the analysis and the context within which they are engaged.

Case Study 1: a Nigerian teacher training college

This is a case study of a teacher training college in Nigeria. In 2002, it had more than 4000 full-time students, 48 per cent of whom were female. The college is divided into Schools, each headed by a Dean. It is run by a senior management team headed by the Provost. It has a Governing Council which oversees policy in the college, and an Academic Board, which is the decision-making body for academic affairs. All teaching and administrative posts are appointed by the Provost (with the exception of the Deans who are usually elected).

Even a superficial glance reveals a highly gendered organisation: female students and female staff are in the majority, but men hold almost all positions of responsibility. Most of the female staff (approximately 65 per cent of the total) work in secretarial, support, and junior teaching roles. Female lecturers are clustered in a few subjects, in particular home economics, fine arts, and education. This general impression suggests that a structured gender analysis of activities and roles among both staff and students would be very illuminating. Given that the gendered nature of organisations stems from behaviour that is informal, unofficial, and largely not commented on verbally or in documentation, it is important here to distinguish between formal and informal roles and responsibilities. The following activity profile is therefore divided into formal and informal roles and responsibilities of staff and students.

Activity profile

This should be divided into appropriate categories: here into male and female staff and students. If the purpose or focus of the gender analysis was different, the categories might also have been different: for example, academic staff and administrative staff, or management and teaching staff.

Formal roles and responsibilities

Staff: the Governing Council consists of eleven members, of whom only two are women. The senior management team responsible for policy, finance, personnel, and administration is all male. Only one of the Deans is female, and she found herself in this position by default, as no alternative (male) candidate was available. She heads the School of Vocational Education, which offers agriculture, home economics, fine arts, and business studies. Out of more than 30 Heads of Department, only six are female. Most of the administrative staff, who work to the orders of senior staff, are female. In addition to their teaching role, female lecturers serve as matrons in the student hostels. For men, the main additional role to teaching is chairing committees. Only two of the Standing Committees – those concerned with student discipline and advice – are headed by women, but almost all have female secretaries.

Students: within the student body, presidents of the Students' Union have traditionally been male and their vice-presidents female. The financial secretary and the treasurer have also usually been female; it seems that they are trusted more by the student body. Most student clubs and committees are headed by men.

Informal roles and responsibilities

Staff: in the daily life of the college, outside their formal teaching role, women carry out duties that are primarily an extension of their domestic and caring functions in the home, that is, those that involve the servicing of men. In staff meetings, the secretaries are always women, and women staff serve the refreshments, even when junior male staff are present and could carry out this duty. The chairpersons are always men. Women staff act *in loco parentis* with regard to students, offering advice and counselling. The newly established counselling centre is headed by a woman.

Male members of staff play sports: football, basketball, and volleyball. Only two female staff members play sports regularly (volleyball and handball). Male staff are much more likely to have opportunities to interact and network in ways which give them an advantage over women in terms of informal access to information and to those in positions of authority. This may come about because they are able to spend more time on the college campus than women, whose day may be tightly organised around domestic duties.

Students: outside their studies, male students usually play sport or engage in income generating activities; alternatively they are involved in family matters, for example, receiving guests, settling disputes, disciplining juniors. Again, male students may spend time sharing information in the student cafeteria after classes, while female students are obliged to return home.

These gender-specific roles and responsibilities can be captured in a Harvard **activity chart** (Table 4.6). This has been modified to distinguish between organisational (productive) roles, home (both reproductive and productive), and community roles, as it is clear that in the Nigerian context for both women and men their roles in the home and the community are related to the roles that they take on, or are given, in the workplace. As explained above, it may be that other categorisations are more relevant in other settings. Before and after the college day, women usually have to cook, do domestic work, and take care of children. After work, they may have to take their children to the hospital or do some farming. Some male staff give private tutorials for extra money after the college day (and sometimes also during working hours), or farm, engage in local politics, or sit on local government committees. Activities and responsibilities outside the college have an impact on what women and men do during college hours.

Table 4.6 Activity profile of staff and student roles in the college

	Female staff	Male staff	Female students	Male students
College roles	Teaching Taking minutes of meetings, acting as committee secretaries Some heads of department, secretaries, and cleaners	Teaching Chairing committees Senior management Most heads of department	Serving refreshments and entertaining guests at special occasions (graduation, etc.)	Chairing student committees and clubs Representing students in the Students' Union and as class representatives
Home roles	Domestic duties, caring for children Farming	Private tutoring Farming Running businesses such as 'business centres' and shops	Helping with domestic chores Some help in farming and marketing	Engaging in income generating activities Disciplining juniors Farming
Community roles	Organising / supporting social events (births, weddings, funerals)	Visiting friends Political activity Leisure activities	Limited public role Obedient and respectful attitudes to the community	Help in maintaining law and order

Table 4.7 Access and control profile for college staff

	Access		Control	
Resources	**Female staff**	**Male staff**	**Female staff**	**Male staff**
Capital	No (only for top management)	Yes (top management)	No	Yes (if top management)
Budgets	Only for heads of dept. and dean	Only for heads of dept. and above		Yes (if head of dept or above)
Equipment (vehicles, telephones, etc.)	Very limited (senior management only)	For senior management	Very limited	Yes (if senior management)
Training / staff development (conferences, courses, etc.)	Yes (but less likely to secure funds)	Yes	Limited by family obligations (not free to travel)	Yes
Time	Limited by domestic responsibilities	Yes	Limited by domestic responsibilities	Yes
Curriculum	Less choice of which courses to teach	Given first choice of which courses to teach	Only if head of dept. (but males may still insist)	Head of dept. and above
Support (secretarial, etc.)	Limited (only heads of depts. and above)	If in senior position	Limited (only if senior management)	Yes (if senior management)
Benefits				
Loans (for car, housing, furniture)	Limited, dependent on rank	Yes	No	Yes
External income (tutoring, etc.)	Limited opportunity	Yes	No	Yes
Political power / prestige	Very limited (men are closer to senior management)	Yes	No	Yes
Promotion	Severely constrained by opportunity; vulnerable to discrimination	Yes	No	Yes
Perks, legal or illegal (e.g. bonus payments, sexual favours from students)	Not close enough to senior management for trips and discretionary payments	Yes	No	Yes

44 | *Practising Gender Analysis in Education*

Access and control profile

Leading on from the activity profile, the access and control profile shown in Table 4.7 covers staff only in the college, but a similar one could be done for students. The same categories of resources and benefits have been kept as in the original framework, but the sub-categories have been altered by the researcher to suit the college context. If the Harvard framework was being used in a participatory mode, a brainstorming session could be used to identify the most relevant sub-categories for analysis.

Resources

It can be seen from Table 4.7 that the lack of representation of women in senior positions in a male-dominated organisation has a considerable impact on both their access to and control of resources. Women staff may have access to resources in principle (scholarships, for example) and hence to the benefits, but they are not in control of these resources, and therefore the extent to which they enjoy the benefits is likely to be limited by comparison with men.

Behind the formal display of resources and benefits as revealed in the chart, other informal forces are at work: the more subtle aspects of the 'glass ceiling' that prevents women from moving upward. These are not easily portrayed in a table, but the table itself can be used as a tool to stimulate discussion of the issues in greater depth. Discussion among staff based on the activity and access and control profiles will bring a greater understanding of the barriers that women face, and perhaps generate a willingness by senior management to introduce mechanisms to reduce these. For example, in the case of promotion, female lecturers usually have to do more than men if they are to succeed (to publish more, to sit on more committees, for example). In some cases their promotion or appointment to a senior position is blocked on some excuse. The male senior management knows that women are less likely than men to protest or be difficult if their application for promotion is not successful. The male-dominated culture means that senior management prefers to promote men, so that their meetings can be conducted more at ease.

Even men in junior positions are better placed than women to lobby for resources or preferential treatment. They are more likely to be given access to senior management and will be more confident about confronting them on issues. Female lecturers who complain about unfair treatment may find their way forward blocked. Although clear procedures exist on promotions, the Provost (always a man) can manipulate them with ease. It is worth noting that this college is also subject to much ethnic tension, as is the state of Nigeria currently. Gender is not seen as problematic in the same way as ethnicity, so decisions may be taken to accommodate ethnic sensitivities rather than gender sensitivities. This is an example of where ethnicity cuts across gender and therefore needs to be incorporated into the analysis, if a comprehensive and accurate picture of the gender dynamics of the organisation is to be provided.

Benefits

A category of benefit that emerged from the gender analysis was 'perks'. While some perks may be official, (*per diems*, travel allowances, etc.) they may not be given out equitably. Others perks are unofficial. These unofficial benefits were only included in the chart because the researcher had investigated informal as well as formal activities and roles in the college. As a result, the further sub-category of 'perks' was added to capture those socially unacceptable and hidden features which may not emerge from a superficial overview, and which may be an embarrassment for participants in a workshop setting to talk about openly. In this college, a particular hidden 'benefit' for male lecturers and male students is access to female students (and possibly also male students). Sexual harassment is rife, and female students are often coerced into relationships with male lecturers, or give in to sexual advances because once under a lecturer's 'protection', other male lecturers and students will leave her alone. There have been incidents in the college of male students beating, and sometimes raping, female students, and of male lecturers demanding sexual favours of female students, sometimes using violence or the threat of violence. In the case of female students entering into sexual relationships with male lecturers (in a cultural environment where female sexual activity outside marriage poses great risk and can even lead to the death penalty), they do so not for money but for protection, as some lecturers use their position of power to intimidate female students with the threat that they will fail them in their exams if they do not give in. A female student who rejects a male lecturer's advances may be victimised with a rigged exam result or may even be prevented from sitting an exam. A student who makes an accusation against a lecturer will be expelled if the case is not proven, so complaints are few. There are increasing cases of lecturers marrying their students, but it is not clear whether coercion or the threat of victimisation plays a part in this.

Table 4.8 identifies some of the factors influencing gender relations in the college. From these, opportunities can be identified, which in turn can lead to the creation of a set of strategies and an action plan. Naila Kabeer's Social Relations Approach (chapter 7) could also be used effectively here.

An action plan could be produced by the group involved in doing the analysis shown in Table 4.8, taking one or more items listed in the four boxes. Using an example of a participatory tool that is featured in chapter 9, the female lecturers could decide to take action to address one of the most blatant sources of sex discrimination: academic promotion. This is listed as a 'political' influencing factor in the 'constraints' column. At a meeting of all interested female faculty, they could discuss and agree on how to tackle this inequity (see Table 4.9).

Table 4.8 Influencing factors, constraints, and opportunities

Influencing factors	Constraints	Opportunities
Socio-economic	Limited access to education for girls Early marriage Male exploitation of staff and students affected by poverty Gender specific roles / structuring Men can spend more time on college tasks; women have domestic and household tasks	Drive for UPE Awareness raising Pressure from international community for gender mainstreaming in all education policies and programmes Pressure to produce sex-disaggregated statistics on educational and economic participation Recent research into gender and education
Political	Men block women's access to power; senior management is all male Discriminatory promotions practice Limited participation of women in decision-making hierarchy Lack of gender oriented policies or equal-opportunities policy in college	Laws exist but need to be enforced College exposure to international scrutiny via funding programmes Government exposed to international pressure to implement gender equality goals Pressure for more women staff in senior positions More successful women in public life and business Human rights agenda Women's advocacy organisations
Cultural	Women's place is in the home Women's role is to serve men Early marriage Men not women are leaders Women seen as inferior / less intelligent Reinforcement of male domination through college Religious beliefs Women as mothers and carers Limited interaction between women and men	NGO involvement in education Increased education Greater acceptance of women in economic role Curriculum reform Research on institutional bias and stereotyping has raised awareness

Table 4.9 Women academics' action plan

Identified objective	Desired outcome	Agreed actions	Who organises	Resources required	Timescale	Who monitors
To pursue equality in academic promotions	Equal or greater numbers of females promoted than males	1 Write to senior management 2 Lobby the females on the Governing Council and Staff Union for support 3 Ask the female Dean to take up their cause 4 Speak out at academic meetings 5 Seek advice on how best to complete their applications 6 If refused promotion, ask for written reasons why 7 If more junior men promoted, ask on what criteria	Elected spokespersons or a committee or working group	Time Some travel expenses	Until next promotion round	Committee or working group

Case Study 2: BRAC in Bangladesh[6]

The Bangladesh Rural Advancement Committee (BRAC) is an internationally renowned NGO. Its mission statement as shown on its website is as follows:

> BRAC works with people whose lives are dominated by extreme poverty, illiteracy, disease and other handicaps. With multifaceted development interventions, BRAC strives to bring about positive change in the quality of life of the poor people of Bangladesh. BRAC firmly believes and is actively involved in promoting human rights, dignity and gender equity through poor people's social, economic, political and human capacity building.

BRAC works through the provision of financial services to the landless poor and marginal farmers, education and training, healthcare and family planning, and community organizing. The main vehicle of its education programme has been the Non Formal Education Programme (NFPE) for eight to ten year-old children, followed later by the Kishor Kishori schools for 11–14 year-olds. BRAC currently has 34,000 schools, mostly in rural areas, which enrol 1.1m children. The NFPE offers a three or sometimes four-year programme. Seventy per cent of pupils in BRAC schools are girls, and 97 per cent of teachers are female; this in a country where the enrolment rate of girls in government primary schools is only 50 per cent, and only 19 per cent of female primary school teachers are female. Eighty-five per cent of rural women are illiterate. At least 90 per cent of children who attend BRAC schools complete the course, compared with 35 per cent in government schools. The number of children who have already graduated from BRAC schools is 2.4m.

The 1997 BRAC annual report refers to four kinds of gender transformation through BRAC schools:

- changes taking place in students as part of a gender-sensitive curriculum and co-curricular activities;
- changes taking place in female staff as a result of values within the BRAC organisation;
- changes taking place among teachers by virtue of their new social roles;
- and those among mothers who come to parents' meetings.

One of its stated aims is to alter the relationship between men and women so that it is more equitable, and to empower women to negotiate their gender needs with men. Engaging in a gender analysis of the NFPE programme will allow us to see whether this aim is being met.

There is insufficient information in the documentation available to complete an activity profile following the Harvard Framework. However, such an exercise based on information from those involved in the programme would provide invaluable insights into, for example, the way in which boys and girls interact with each other in the school, the extent to which the teacher raises awareness of gender issues among pupils, and how parents participate in school meetings (especially as it is usually mothers who attend). Both the activity profile and the access and control profile can also be applied to the administration of BRAC, to establish the extent to which the organisation itself is gender-sensitive. Zeeshan Rahman (1998) suggests that this has not been an easy process: despite considerable efforts and fast-tracking of promising young women into management positions, senior positions are occupied mainly by men and there is a male management culture which de-motivates many female staff.

Access and control profile

The chart shown in Table 4.10 provides a gender-sensitive access and control profile only for teachers in BRAC schools and government primary schools. The categories under 'resources' and 'benefits' are not the same as those selected for the previous case study; they are based on the information provided in the documentation. Again, in a participatory mode they could be identified through a brainstorming process.

This exercise is useful for identifying the strengths and weaknesses of both the BRAC and the government school programme. There are strengths in each, but on the whole for women, BRAC provides a more supportive working environment, with good quality materials and regular training. For women, in particular in rural areas, it provides a source of income and status not usually available. The one-teacher school also offers a friendly and conducive environment for girls. However, the limited training available, the isolation of the teacher from other professionals, and the narrow curriculum present some disadvantages of the BRAC model. So, despite the poor professionalism and accountability which characterises government schools, most female as well as male teachers would prefer to work there, for the higher and more secure salary and the higher status.

Sara Longwe's framework (see chapter 5) could also be used effectively here to determine the extent to which BRAC's claims translated into practice. It would reveal increased access to good quality education for girls, increased conscientisation and participation of women, whether as mothers, teachers, or BRAC staff, and of students in terms of the increased self-esteem and self-confidence of girls and greater respect by boys.

Since 1999, BRAC has introduced a new programme: the Adolescent Peer Organized Network for Girls (APON), which provides girls with training in livelihood skills, leadership development, and raising awareness. This programme trains them in peer-education skills in addition to skills that enable them to organise and facilitate groups. The aim is to develop these girls as community leaders and role models, capable of undertaking community-level campaigns and mobilising adolescents to have a voice in their communities. Awareness raising sessions deal with issues such as abuse and exploitation, birth registration, gender discrimination, their own health, and social and environmental issues that affect them. Sara Longwe's framework could be effectively applied here too, to ascertain the extent to which this programme is leading to real empowerment of women.

Commentary

The two case studies above have shown how this framework can be the starting point for gender-sensitive organisational analysis. In the first case it was used by a researcher as part of the process of conceptualising and categorising his findings; in the second it was applied by the author of this book to a set of documents on BRAC. The framework can, however, be used by any group: by senior management, members of an academic department or a personnel office, or a group of teachers or students, for example. It can be used at the start, in the middle, or at the end of the analysis process. It can be used to assess equal opportunities for both staff and students, not only on the basis of gender but also of race, ethnicity, religion, and so on. It will be particularly effective where sex-disaggregated data are available; if such data are not available, the process of working through the framework may encourage managers to produce them.

In the Nigerian case, the researcher decided to use the categories of female and male staff, and female and male student. He could have decided to separate staff into academic or administrative, or senior management and lecturers, on the grounds that their gendered experiences would be very different. As the analysis and the key features emerged, he could have decided to engage the staff and/or students in a participatory exercise to look at these different categories. In the BRAC case, the strengths of BRAC from both the teacher and the pupil perspectives become apparent when BRAC schools are contrasted with government schools. However, a group of BRAC administrators, facilitators, or teachers might like to look for further opportunities to address gender issues either at the level of staff or of pupils, in which case they would use different categories; they might decide to examine the continuing dominance of men on senior management, for example.

Table 4.10 Access and control profile of teachers in BRAC and government schools

Resources	BRAC NFPE	Access & control by women	Government primary	Access & control by women
	Teachers		**Teachers**	
Work	Preference for women (over 90%), married and local (trusted members of the community) Flexible timetabling (3 hours/day) to fit in with other commitments Supportive working environment	Access	Although almost equal numbers of female and male teachers, a male-dominated working environment Low teacher-contact time High teacher absenteeism, especially males (who have additional jobs)	Almost equal access but not equal participation in school decision making
Salary	Lower salary than government teacher; no tenure, but almost no paid work for women in rural areas	Access & control but may depend on male relative	Higher salary and permanent post Allowances	Difficulty of getting salary paid (corrupt officials)
Training	Short, flexible training (15 days initially) suitable for married women with limited mobility Continuing support (monthly refresher training) from programme organisers / assistants (114 days of training in total) Training in pupil-centred participatory approaches Training not always good quality (and very short)	Access	One year training in Primary Training Institute; not feasible for many women with family responsibilities Theoretical, little practical experience Few opportunities for staff development and in-service training	More difficult access than men
Curriculum materials / pedagogy	Designed specifically for rural children Good quality, durable free textbooks Supporting materials (posters, MEENA video, materials on BRAC website) Focus on women and girls Pupil-centred teaching with small classes Very narrow curriculum (only literacy and numeracy; no science, which constrains opportunities at higher level)	Access & some control of materials	Poorly resourced, only government textbooks, no supplementary materials, often not relevant to rural children Low teacher interaction with pupils due to teacher-centred pedagogy and large classes	Limited

Community	Monthly parents' meeting (80% attend, mostly mothers) School-management committee (3 parents, community leader with the teacher) to take ownership of school	Access & some control through good relations	Little community involvement School seen as separate and unfriendly; slack management Lack of accountability to community	Very limited access
School facilities	Location in the community Small classes 1:33 teacher–pupil ratio Pupil work on display No running water or toilets	Access & some control	Larger building, with toilet facilities and tube well, but poor maintenance Over-crowded classes, 1:60 teacher–pupil ratio Unfriendly; no pupil work on display	Practical difficulties for women / girls
Benefits	**Teachers**			
Income	Little or no available work in rural areas for women, so motivated to keep job They come from the community, know the pupils by name, and visit them at home	Access & control	Higher salary but low performance due to other possible sources of income, e.g. private tutoring (even of own pupils from school), farming, business interests, political activity)	Unequal access and control
Basic needs	Practical: welfare needs (income to buy food, etc.)	Access & control	Pressure on males to fulfil traditional breadwinner role	
Working environment	School close to community, small class size; same class over 3 years allows special bond between pupil and teacher School facilities usually rented by BRAC; landlord responsible for good order School displays pupil work	Access & some control	Male dominated, not friendly Poor support	Unequal access and control
Status	Enhanced status in community Greater self-respect, self-confidence, and independence through income Programme Assistants (supervise teachers and schools) ride cycles and motorbikes – breaking the norms of female roles	Access & some control	Higher status than BRAC school, but within school men have higher status than women	Less than for male teachers

The Harvard Framework | 53

Uses

Planning: this is a good tool for planners. It clearly presents a picture of who does what, when, and with what. It makes women's contribution very visible and shows up the disparities in workloads between men and women. The recognition of the importance of control of as well as access to resources is valuable.

Data collection and analysis: the Harvard Framework is particularly useful for collecting data and analysing projects. It is easy to use. However, it is best used for micro-level analysis.

Organisational analysis: although not explicitly designed for this, it lends itself well.

Training: it is useful for training purposes, especially as a starting point for considerations of gender issues, as it focuses on roles and activities (real situations). It goes well with an analysis of practical and strategic gender needs.

Communication: the framework is based on an economic argument, so economists will feel at ease with it. Development agencies are likely to feel comfortable using it.

Limitations

Narrow focus: the emphasis of the Harvard Framework is on efficiency and roles rather than on equity, identities, relations, and agency. The focus is rather narrow. It is not aimed at gender transformation but at an equitable share of resources, which in itself may not help women. It may even have a negative impact on their livelihoods because it may encourage them to start up economic ventures, for example, by making credit available, which then end in failure.

Gender relations: the framework does not ask how and why gender relations are unequal, and so issues of power are not made explicit. It does not examine relationships between men and women, and so the underlying causes (and their consequences) cannot be examined. However, these can emerge from a discussion of the division of labour, and access and control of resources (as is shown by the Nigerian case study).

Gender strategies: it lacks the hierarchical dimension of Sara Longwe's empowerment framework. It does not give a sense of the extent to which interventions might contribute towards the achievement of strategic gender goals.

Using the profiles: it can be simplistic if it is used just to tick boxes. This will distort the reality and under-estimate the complexity of most situations. It may be difficult to fill in if there is confusion over what should go into the resources table and what into the benefits table. With access and control analysis, access can be determined relatively easily but control is much more complex and likely to be gained in incremental stages. This is difficult to convey in the chart.

Participation: the Harvard Framework is not automatically a participatory tool. It is likely to be used in a top-down manner by planners without much consultation with the supposed beneficiaries.

Further reading

Rahman, Zeeshan H. (1998) 'Non-formal primary education: a gender-based programme', in P. Drake and P. Owen *Gender and Management Issues in Education: an International Perspective*, Trentham Books, pp. 67–77.

Nath, S.R. (2002) 'The transition from Non-Formal to Formal education: the case of BRAC, Bangladesh', *International Review of Education*, 48(6): 517–24.

5 | Women's Empowerment Framework (Longwe)

Introduction

The Women's Empowerment Framework was developed by Sara Longwe, a consultant on gender and development based in Zambia. It is explained in detail in the *Oxfam Gender Training Manual* (1995) and Tina Wallace and Candida March's book (1991) *Changing Perceptions: Writings on Gender and Development*. Sara Longwe has also written about gender and education: she argues that the existing school system contributes to women's subordination, and so lack of schooling cannot be seen as a major cause of women's low socio-economic status. Education for women's empowerment requires a very different model, one in which the participants think and work collectively, question the social and political environment, and develop strategies which will allow them to work in an area of political conflict and confrontation where there is no consensus about policies for gender equality (Longwe 1998).

Although designed for women's empowerment (its failure to use *gender* as the defining concept has been criticised), there seems to be no reason why it could not be used for other disadvantaged groups as well, for example, marginalised men, ethnic minority groups, disabled people. It can easily be applied to educational settings.

Basic principles

This framework is intended to help policy makers, planners, managers, and evaluators assess the extent to which a policy, organisation, or programme is committed to women's empowerment, and if so, to what kind of empowerment and with what impact. Empowerment in this context is intended to mean the achievement of equal participation in and control of the development process and its benefits by men and women. It means enabling women to take greater control of their own lives. It encourages gender awareness in development projects, and helps develop the ability to recognise women's issues, whether in projects that involve only women or those that involve both women and men.

This framework can be used at any stage of the project or programme cycle: at the planning or design stage, for monitoring purposes during implementation, or for final evaluation. The first case study below from Tanzania draws on a primary education project to show how an application of Longwe's framework at the earliest planning stage could have resulted in a more gender-sensitive project, and this in turn would have made it easier for the project to meet its objectives.

Sara Longwe's framework is based on the notion of five different levels of equality, shown in Table 5.1. The extent to which these five levels of equality are present in any area of social or economic life determines the level of empowerment. This is measured in two ways:

a) assessing which levels of equality are addressed by a particular intervention;

b) assessing which levels of recognition of women's issues exist in the project/programme/organisation's objectives.

The levels of equality are hierarchical, in that project or programme aims that focus on the higher levels are more likely to bring about women's empowerment than those focused on the lower levels. In other words, equality of participation or control between men and women is more likely to bring about significant change than equality of welfare or access. Equal welfare or access is not empowering in itself: one needs conscientisation (awareness of the need for change and of the means to achieve it), participation in the change process, and preferably control of the process if change is to be sustained. This links up with the Harvard Framework explained in chapter 4, which distinguishes between activities (participation) and (access and) control of the resources needed to engage in the activities. The Harvard Framework does not, however, place them in a hierarchy.

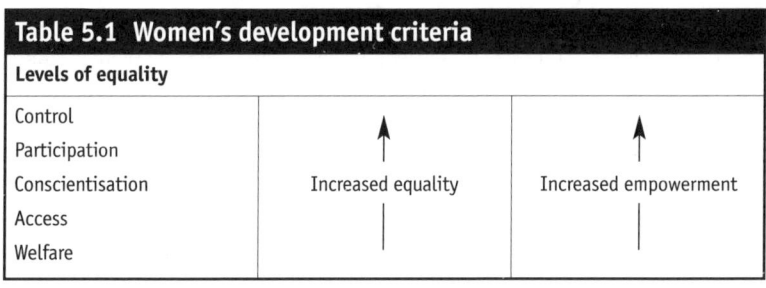

Table 5.1 Women's development criteria

Levels of equality		
Control		
Participation	↑	↑
Conscientisation	Increased equality	Increased empowerment
Access		
Welfare		

Source: Longwe, in Wallace and March 1991: 151

Levels of equality: definitions

Welfare

This is the level of women's material welfare relative to men (equal access to food, income, and shelter). It is less relevant to education but might be a factor when welfare is used as an encouragement to get girls into school, for example, free school meals, free uniforms, and scholarships in some countries, such as Bangladesh and Pakistan. Unequal pay for female and male teachers exists in some countries.

Access

This is defined as equal access to the factors of production: land, labour, credit, education and training, marketing, and all public services and benefits. This level relates to equal opportunities and the need to remove all forms of legal and administrative discrimination against women. Access to education, particularly at the higher levels, is often very unequal, with many more girls than boys in the poorest countries denied any education at all, or not permitted to go beyond the primary level. At the junior secondary level, there may be limited places for girls, or boys may be allocated the majority of available places.

Conscientisation

This is the conscious understanding of the difference between sex and gender, and an awareness that gender roles, including the sexual division of labour, are culturally determined and can be changed. Although schools should develop an awareness of the importance of fair distribution of labour, and lead by example, in fact they usually reinforce gendered practices by the allocation of duties to female and male staff and students on the basis of stereotypical views of what is appropriate. This was referred to in chapter 1.

Participation

This refers to equal participation in decision making, whether in policy making, planning, or administration. Within a project context, this could mean involvement in needs assessment, project formulation, implementation, or evaluation. It requires involvement of the women of the community affected by the decisions taken. Within a school setting, this relates to ensuring equality of opportunity for both staff and students, whether in terms of subject or career choices for students, staff-development opportunities and promotion procedures, or equal voice for students in the classroom, in extra-curricular activities, and in school affairs.

Control

This is defined as equal control over decision making, including the factors of production and the distribution of benefits. It means a balance of control between women and men, so that neither side dominates. This is related to the above point about participation: participants in schooling need to have equal control of what they are entitled to, for example, a female head of department should have the same level of control as a male head over departmental budgets and other resources, and over decision making within the department; there should be equal numbers of female and male students as prefects or representatives on student committees, with equal responsibilities.

The first two of these levels of equality (welfare and access) primarily address women's practical gender needs, and the following three levels address women's strategic gender needs. However, Longwe recognises that the separation of practical and strategic is not helpful, as most development interventions have elements of both. Satisfying a practical gender need has an impact on strategic needs. It is also important to note that an intervention does not need to start with activities at the welfare level and work up through each level. It could be located at a higher level, according to its objectives. However, a project will not be successful if it is excessively ambitious and erroneously assumes that women have already achieved certain levels of equality, such as access to resources or conscientisation. The case study from India which features in chapter 6 is an example of a project which sought to move a group of women almost overnight from being among the poorest and most disadvantaged in Indian society to being independent entrepreneurs exercising considerable control over their lives. Not surprisingly, it failed. In an educational context, an attempt to appoint female managers only in a system where there are currently very few experienced female teachers from whose ranks promotions may be made, and where women are generally perceived as inferior to men, is unlikely to succeed in the short term. Some element of conscientisation and participation may be achieved, but little will shift in the balance of control.

Levels of recognition

It is also important to identify the level of recognition of women's issues in the objectives of a particular project or programme. The level of empowerment achieved by an intervention is dependent on the extent to which its objectives address women's issues (whether at the level of welfare, access, conscientisation, participation, or control). Longwe identifies three levels of recognition:

Negative: no mention made of women's issues

Neutral: recognition of women's issues but not really addressed

Positive: project objectives are aimed at improving women's position relative to men.

In some projects, for example, the objectives may have potentially different outcomes for men and women, but if these have not been identified, there is a negative level of recognition. In others the objectives may be gender-specific, but there is no strategy to address them separately (neutral level). In some, the strategy may be gender-sensitive (positive level).

Application to educational settings

Sara Longwe's framework is very flexible and can be applied to any type of intervention that seeks to improve the social, economic, and political conditions of women (or other disadvantaged groups) in whatever setting. In education, it can be applied to a policy (for example on basic education), a formal or non-formal education or training programme (such as literacy or vocational training) or a curriculum. Its use in needs assessment allows for the development of project or programme objectives and strategies to improve the situation of women (or other groups). One curriculum example might be to apply the five levels of equality to a set of learning materials, which may show that women and girls are portrayed as being equal only at the level of welfare or access, but at the level of participation and control only men and boys are portrayed. A revised set of materials might seek to ensure that girls and women are portrayed as being equal partners in decision-making and in control of resources.

Here, Oxfam's Tanzania Primary Education Project and ActionAid's *Reflect* programme in Ghana provide case studies for the application of Longwe's framework. Although still retaining the focus on women's empowerment, the framework is applied within a gender context.

Case Study 1: the Tanzania Primary Education Project

This commentary provides an assessment of the extent to which this Oxfam project is likely to address gender goals, based on an analysis of the project proposal. The project is located within the Tanzanian government's Education Sector Development Programme. It is interesting to note that the government's 2002–6 Primary Education Development Plan contains no recognition at all that access, retention, and quality issues may be different for girls and boys, nor does it provide any sex-disaggregated statistics. This is despite the government's commitment to the international goals on EFA (as have been detailed in chapter 1). The source document is the Tanzania Primary Education Project, Oxfam, 1999.[7]

The stated **aim** of this project is to raise the standard of living of people in some of the poorest communities in Tanzania through

- improving the quality of education in selected primary schools in one region;
- improving access and retention;

- encouraging good governance and accountability at community and school level;
- and improving responsiveness of local government to local realities and needs.

It is intended as a community-based participatory intervention, initially working with ten schools and communities and ultimately with 60. **Indicators** identified to achieve this aim are:

- improved enrolment rates;
- primary school leaving exam pass rates and completion rates;
- increased public attendance at meetings and popular approval of community-based committees.

The main **outputs** are intended to be:

- strengthened school and community management including accountability;
- school environments made conducive to learning;
- appropriate and sufficient learning opportunities made available in school;
- improvements in the teaching and learning processes;
- increased activity and capacity of government officials to support school development.

Communities in which the schools are located will provide labour to build or renovate classrooms and to construct latrines, as well as make contributions in cash and kind.

As part of the project planning stage, a **situational analysis** was generated, which according to the project document used a participatory process: 'all stakeholders were involved in identifying key issues and problems' (Oxfam 1999: 11). The analysis identifies five major problems facing schools:

- a poor school environment, not conducive to education;
- a shortage of teaching materials and equipment;
- problems with the teaching staff in terms of morale, attitude, status, numbers, and training;
- truancy of pupils, related to discipline issues, child labour, and poverty;
- ineffective school management, including accountability to the community.

The only **gender-specific issues** identified by the situational analysis are:

- weak female representation on community committees, which are dominated by (male) government officials;
- the difficulty of deploying female teachers to rural areas. Some rural schools have no female teachers, which deprives girls of positive role models and a source of advice on issues such as health and HIV (male teachers said they felt uncomfortable dealing with grown-up girls);

- truancy and drop-out among girls due to increased domestic roles or early marriage, and among boys due to herding. However, the analysis considered that most causes of truancy (estimated to be on average 20 per cent at the time of the field work) were not gender-specific. General causes were identified as: the low quality of education, child labour, poverty, the high level of contributions expected of parents, and the excessive use of corporal punishment. Pupils saw school as largely irrelevant.

It is clear that the emphasis in this project is on *improved access* (of pupils to an effective school learning environment), *conscientisation* (of the community to the importance of education and to their involvement in local provision), and *participation* (of the community through school contributions, greater involvement in school affairs through committees, and decision-making). It can be expected that strengthened village committees and community management will also lead to *greater control* of the school by the community.

However, when we look closely at the context within which these objectives and outputs are articulated, it appears that there are many complex issues that go beyond the need for resources or improved management. The social dimension, including the construction of gender, needs to be unpacked and addressed if the project is to be successful. Applying Longwe's framework would allow the planners to identify the extent to which the project as it is formulated will address issues of gender, both in terms of the level of gender equality and empowerment and of the level of recognition in the objectives. When using the information provided in the project document, we find that in fact there is very little which addresses women's or girls' needs specifically. It is therefore in Longwe's terminology 'gender negative' (gender-unaware, according to the terminology used in this book). Table 5.2 looks at this level by level.

Longwe's levels of recognition of women's issues show us that at each level of gender equality this project's objectives (and therefore its outputs) are at best 'gender neutral'. There is only a very vague recognition of the need to address gender roles and needs, and very little attempt to identify gender-related problems, despite statements of the commitment that 'gender roles and needs will be addressed throughout the project cycle' and that the project will 'take a proactive interest in gender concerns'. There are numerous references in the project document to training in gender-sensitivity for project staff, school committees, and teachers 'as required' and to gender concerns being 'integrated' into initial awareness raising in project schools and other interventions. It is not at all clear what exactly will be addressed or how, however, as the logical framework and the draft work plan in the project proposal provide no gender-specific outputs, no identified needs, and no activities apart from gender training. There is only a general commitment to the goal of gender equality, and the opportunity has been missed to identify

Table 5.2 Levels of equality and recognition of gender issues

Level of gender equality	Extent to which gender is addressed	Level of recognition of gender issues
Welfare	Only addressed indirectly, insofar as the long-term aim of the project is to improve the standard of living of the community through providing a better education for young people, so that they can get jobs or engage in successful income generation.	Negative: no gender-differentiation in education and employment
Access	Educational access for children will be improved by constructing or renovating classrooms, improving the school environment, school management, and the teaching and learning process.	Negative / neutral: some recognition of girls' and women's needs
Conscientisation	Awareness raising regarding the need for strong school and community leadership and community mobilisation and facilitation is planned. Training of school and village committees, training in gender sensitivity for relevant groups, and meetings between parents, teachers, and pupils will be encouraged so as to raise awareness and increase openness and accountability.	Negative / neutral: does recognise the need for greater female representation on committees but not clear how to achieve it
Participation	Quality of teaching and learning will be improved by strengthening school and community leadership, management, and accountability. Participation by parents, teachers, and other community members crucial. Acknowledgement that women are under-represented in the decision-making process but very little understanding of underlying causes, and its consequences.	Negative / neutral: some recognition of under-representation of women
Control	Greater control of the school by the community through strengthened committees, but government officials are still in overall charge.	Negative: women poorly represented

gender issues during the needs-assessment stage, and to develop gender-specific objectives. It is unlikely therefore that gender-equality issues will be addressed, given that the stated aim, the identified problems, the intended outputs, and the indicators of success do not differentiate at all on gender grounds.

Applying the Longwe framework at the planning stage would help to operationalise the concept of empowerment and make concrete the expressions of intent regarding gender. Without this, there is a risk that the project will bring no benefits to women or girls, and may even be detrimental to their needs. It may also fail to meet boys' needs, as their truancy and dropout seem to be poorly understood. Alternatively, where it does bring benefits, they will be incidental rather than the outcome of a specific strategy, and therefore it will not be possible to identify a cause-and-effect link between objectives, activities, and outputs.

Using a gender analysis framework ensures that gender needs and roles can be clearly identified, addressed, and monitored; in this case in terms of girls' and boys' access, retention, and achievement in education, conscientisation of the community regarding women's roles, and women's own conscientisation (greater valuing of oneself and one's contribution, awareness of gender constraints, and possibly a willingness to challenge them). Some of the PRA tools described in chapter 9 could be used constructively here, for example, a time line or matrix to register and monitor change, or a problem wall to identify barriers to improved access or conscientisation. By making gender explicit, not only will gender equality be directly addressed, but also project goals are more likely to be achieved. This would allow for appropriate indicators to be set which reflect gender equity targets.

Table 5.3 provides examples of the kinds of questions that could usefully be asked at the situational analysis and planning stage of the project of community members, teachers, parents, and children, as well as of ministry officials and politicians, using Sara Longwe's framework. The findings of this process could then help formulate the project objectives. To do this effectively requires gathering sex-disaggregated data, which are largely absent here.

Using a gender framework helps clarify such issues by looking at their different impact on boys and girls. It would also make clear whether the project is addressing practical needs (access) or strategic needs (participation and control). By raising these questions, we begin to see that what on the surface looks like a simple set of objectives and outputs, requiring mainly the input of financial and human resources, is in fact very complicated and requires traditional gender roles to be challenged by asking, for example, who pays for what; who makes what decisions in the household; why?

The Harvard framework could also be used here to identify issues of access and control, as well as influencing factors, constraints, and opportunities. The Gender Analysis Matrix could be used as a monitoring tool.

Table 5.3 Improving levels of recognition of gender-issues

Level of equality	Extent to which gender is addressed	Level of recognition
Welfare	Will education benefit girls and boys differently? If so, how? How can it be made more relevant to their needs? How will it increase their access to jobs? Does it require a different curriculum?	Positive
Access	Are girls disadvantaged in terms of access, and if so, how? Are boys also disadvantaged but differentially? What are the causes and patterns of truancy of girls and boys? Are they different? At what stage do girls and boys drop out? What can be done to address this? Do factors such as lack of clean latrines and water, lack of desks (pupils sit on the floor), and corporal punishment deter girls more than boys? Is pregnancy and early marriage a major cause of girls' drop-out? If yes, how can this be addressed? What deters female teachers from teaching in the community? Is it important to have female teachers in the schools? Why? How can more be recruited and retained?	Positive
Conscientisation	Do adult women and men value education, and the education of girls and boys, differently? Why? How do men and women regard issues of equal representation in the community? How do teachers treat boys and girls? What do boys and girls learn at school about gender roles and relations? Women carry the main burden of paying school contributions in Tanzania – why is this so, and should it be changed?	Positive
Participation	How many women sit on committees? How are committee members selected? Is it important that more women are involved? What would allow them to participate more? How does the committee function/how are decisions taken? When and where are meetings held? Does this disadvantage women?	Positive
Control	If women make a greater financial contribution to the school, do they have control over these resources and decide what to give to the school? How many women fill leadership roles? If not many, what are the barriers to this?	Positive

Case Study 2: The *Reflect* programme in Ghana

Reflect is an innovative approach to adult literacy developed by the UK-based NGO ActionAid, which combines Freirean theory on literacy with PRA methodology. It was piloted in 1993–5 in three countries, Uganda, El Salvador, and Bangladesh, and has since then been used in many countries and many languages. In 2000, the International Reflect Circle (CIRAC) was set up as a forum 'to promote the solidarity of *Reflect* practitioners at different levels around the world in order to strengthen international exchange and learning, and build a wider movement' (Global Survey of Reflect 2001: 2). It now has links to 350 organisations using *Reflect* in 61 countries.

Typically, *Reflect* has been used in rural communities, especially with women. It often builds on existing groups such as women's groups, literacy groups, and rotating credit groups. *Reflect* groups are organised into 'circles'. Each literacy circle develops its own learning materials through the construction of maps, matrices, calendars, time lines, and diagrams that represent local reality. These are usually created first on the ground using available materials (sticks, stones, beans, etc.), with a local facilitator supporting the discussion. This is usually directed at identifying local needs and issues. These drawings are then transferred to large sheets of paper and words are introduced which are meaningful in the particular context described in the graphics. There are no textbooks or primers, only a guide for facilitators. In this way, the group builds up its own learning materials based on its own local reality, over which it can feel strong ownership. As the course progresses, the participants produce a large number of graphics with accompanying words, thus developing a widening vocabulary. These materials form a permanent record for communities and a basis on which to plan their own development. This is a form of participatory needs analysis or appraisal, which raises awareness of the participants' own circumstances and inspires them to take ownership of the issues raised, at the same time as providing them with literacy skills.

This approach contrasts sharply with that of conventional literacy programmes, where adults are often taught by school teachers working after school hours or in vacation time, with lessons being held in schools or other public buildings. They usually teach in the same didactic way as in school in a manner that is found patronising by adult learners, using primers which are often of poor quality and whose content bears little meaningful relation to their own circumstances. Drop-out from literacy programmes is often very high after a few weeks because they fail to engage the learners. A more learner-centred approach, which claims to build on the learners' own experiences and to teach them what they want to know, is much more likely to be motivating.

> **Box 1 Activities of a *Reflect* literary circle, Ghana**
> - Gender relations: Selection of two women participants as community leaders. One woman participant also took responsibility as school cook (previously a problem). Men were reported to take some advice from women, e.g. selling livestock when prices were high during the year.
> - Post-harvest storage: explained as women persuading men not to sell the surplus but to store it for the family.
> - Planted trees along the river for protection.
> - Planted grass to prevent erosion.
> - Talked of improved sanitation (as in facilitator's guide) but no evidence of action.
> - Regraded road without the use of machinery. This consisted of mobilising the community to fill holes, move stones, and cut grass. The condition of the road was observed to be better than before.
> - Increased enrolment at nearby primary school, and participants declared their increased commitment to help their children attend school and not drop out.
> - Gender: One man had agreed a work contract with his wife, on condition he was still recognised as head of household. This could be the start of a trend.
> - More crop diversification to prepare for the hungry season (more food crops).

Although *Reflect* was originally conceived as a radical new approach to adult literacy and empowerment, it has evolved into an approach that focuses more generally on communication practices and empowerment. Many organisations use *Reflect* purely as a participatory and empowering learning process without the literacy component. The approach engages people in reflection and self-analysis of their socio-economic, cultural, and political environment with a view to initiating change. Because of this, and the focus on process, it facilitates the identification and recognition of diversity and power imbalances between individuals and groups in their own community and in the wider society.

Despite the high level of women's participation in *Reflect* programmes and the acknowledged aim of community empowerment, group evaluations of their achievements are surprisingly non-gendered. One example of a literacy circle which includes an element of gender analysis in its activities is provided by *Reflect*, Ghana. These activities are summarised in Box 1.[8]

The list in Box 1 presents a mixture of activities, impacts, and observations. It is difficult to identify how particular activities might have led to particular impacts without a systematic analysis. Using Sara Longwe's five levels as illustrated, we can see that there is

- improved welfare (through learning to diversify crops);
- improved participation by women in community affairs (two women being chosen as community leaders);

- improved participation by some women in household decision making (some men taking advice or being persuaded as to when to sell livestock and when not to sell surplus grain);
- and one case of a woman who is securing an element of control over her life (negotiating a work contract with her husband). In another circle, one man said that he cooked when his wife went to market – and didn't care if he was laughed at.

Table 5.4 Ghana *Reflect* programme – achievements

Levels of equality	Individual	Household	Community	Comments
Control	One woman negotiated a work contract with her husband			
Participation	Two women as community leaders	Advising men on when to sell livestock Persuading men not to sell surplus grain		
Conscientisation	Yes (but how / what?)	Yes (but how / what?)	Yes (but how / what?)	
Access	Opportunity for children to go to school	More commitment to schooling	Increased enrolments at primary school	
Welfare	More food through crop diversification	More food	More food Less erosion (who planted grass and trees?) Regraded road (who?)	

If a gender analysis framework had been used systematically during the evaluation of the circle's activities, this would have allowed for a more rigorous discussion of gender roles and of the achievements of women and men along all five levels. This would have indicated who benefited from which achievements (Which women? Which men? Which children? Who had been conscientised? What were the outcomes?); and who carried out the physical labour required by these initiatives. It would also have allowed for the identification of work still to be done, and an action plan or strategy for further activity could have been drawn up. As Table 5.4 illustrates, there are a number of gaps that a comprehensive gender analysis would have filled.

It might also have made it more difficult for dubious claims to be made about what has been achieved and about the sustainability of what the circle was doing. Fiedrich and Jellema (2003), for example, probed into exactly what changes *Reflect* circles had made to the lives of participants on some programmes, and found that it was far less than was claimed. Sometimes claims of 'empowerment' were made which in fact were just logical responses to changing circumstances.

Commentary

Uses

The framework is simple to use and flexible. It can be used in many different contexts.

Planning, monitoring, and evaluation: Longwe's framework can be used for planning and policy making, monitoring of project or programme implementation, and evaluation. It allows those involved to assess the objectives in terms of gender equality, and to identify the nature and level of their input in terms of women's empowerment (or of other aims).

Empowerment: It focuses on empowerment and what it means in real development (or education) contexts. It therefore has transformatory potential. It can be used to examine what kind of empowerment is involved in a particular project or programme. This can then easily be linked to the identification of practical and/or strategic gender needs.

Impact assessment: It helps identify the gap between reality and rhetoric, because it requires an examination of particular aspects of individual or collective lives and a measurement of how much has been achieved against the five levels. (Many initiatives only reach the level of conscientisation, and stakeholders can easily assume that much more has been achieved.) For this reason, it lends itself well to gender training purposes.

Limitations

Measuring change: It is rather basic. It is static – a 'snapshot' – and cannot easily record changes over time.

Equality: It is uni-dimensional and only looks at equality issues. It does not look at other forms of inequality. It is difficult to incorporate other indicators of inequality such as race or ethnicity in the analysis. It is therefore also not suited to macro-analyses.

Lack of complexity: It deals with generalities. This could be misleading as it then downplays the complexities in any given situation. It is not appropriate for organisational or institutional analysis.

Gender relations: It focuses on women only rather than on gender relations (although there is no reason why it cannot be applied to other disadvantaged groups just as effectively). This can encourage a view of women's issues as separate from men and without an understanding of either gender relations or men's needs and interests.

Impact assessment: The hierarchy of levels gives the impression that there is a linear progression up the levels, which is not the case. It is a fairly crude measurement which does not differentiate between degrees of impact.

Further reading

Fiedrich, M. and A. Jellema (2003) *Literacy, Gender and Social Agency: Adventures in Empowerment,* London: DFID.

Longwe, S. (1998) 'Education for women's empowerment or schooling for women's subordination?', in *Gender and Development,* 6(2): 19–26.

Longwe, S. (1991) 'Gender awareness: the missing element in the Third World development project', in T. Wallace and C. March *Changing Perceptions: Writings on Gender and Development.* Oxford: Oxfam, pp. 149–57.

6 | Gender Analysis Matrix

Introduction

This tool is different from the other frameworks in that it measures impact over time – it does more than take a snapshot of a situation at one particular point in time. Its author, Rani Parker, designed it to be used by development practitioners (originally in the Middle East) rather than by policy makers and planners, and intended it to be used in a participatory format. It can be relatively easily adapted to educational settings. The method is explained by the author, A. Rani Parker, in her training manual *Another Point of View: a Manual on Gender Analysis Training for Grassroots Workers* (1993).

Basic principles

Rani Parker created the Gender Analysis Matrix (GAM) to serve two purposes:

- to provide a community-based technique for the identification and analysis of gender differences in order to assess the different impact of development interventions on men and women;
- to initiate a process of analysis that identifies and challenges in a constructive manner assumptions about gender roles within the community.

By separating out the different impact on women and men, the GAM helps development practitioners to accommodate different needs and interests. Unlike more traditional methods of analysis, it does not begin with an assessment of the current situation. Instead, it enables the community to articulate a full range of expectations concerning a particular project at the start, so that over time, the likelihood of changes favouring gender equity is increased. The author also identifies three basic principles underlying the Matrix:

- All requisite knowledge for gender analysis exists among the people whose lives are the subject of analysis.
- Gender analysis does not require the technical expertise of those outside the community being analysed, except as facilitators.
- Gender analysis cannot be transformative unless the analysis is done by the people being analysed.

Like participatory rural appraisal (PRA), the GAM is intended to serve as a participatory tool in which the participants carry out the information gathering and analysis themselves in a forum which allows both women and men to put forward their own perspective, to appreciate that of others, and to learn from the process. In this way, a programme can be developed which is gender-sensitive and responsive to particular circumstances, and is more likely to lead to genuine and sustainable change.

Both men and women (preferably in equal numbers) should be engaged in the task. If it is inappropriate that they work in mixed sex groups, they can meet first separately and then, if possible, together. This applies also to children: if one sex (usually girls) is lacking in self-confidence, they can first work separately and then share their perspectives once they have talked them through.

The GAM can be used at the planning, design, monitoring, or evaluation stages of a project or programme. At the planning stage it can help determine whether potential gender effects are desirable and consistent with project or programme aims. At the design stage, it may influence changes as a consequence of gender considerations. At the monitoring and evaluation stages, it can help assess broader project or programme impacts beyond that of the immediate stated objectives (Parker 1993: 24, 47). It is a dynamic tool and can be used periodically to verify expected impacts and identify unexpected results so that they can be addressed. The recommended strategy is that the analysis should be reviewed and revised once a month for the first three months, and once every three months thereafter. Unexpected results must be added to the Matrix. If it is part of a project or programme, it should be used in addition to other standard tools of analysis such as monitoring tools and needs assessments (*ibid.*: 27).

The original GAM as shown in Figure 2 has four **levels of analysis** appearing vertically on the Matrix, and four **categories of analysis** appearing horizontally on the Matrix, to be applied at each level of analysis.

Levels of analysis

Women: this refers to women of all ages who are in the target group (if the target group includes women) or to all women in the community.
Men: this refers to men of all ages who are in the target group (if the target group includes men) or to all men in the community.

Figure 2: Gender Analysis Matrix				
	Labour	Time	Resources	Culture
Women				
Men				
Household				
Community				
	1 Are the effects listed above desirable? Are they consistent with programme goals? 2 How will this activity affect those who do not participate? 3 Unexpected results – to be dentified during implementation			

Source: Parker 1993: 38

Household: this refers to all women, men, and children residing together, even if they are not part of one nuclear family. Although the types of household may vary even within the same community, people always know what constitutes their 'household' or 'family'.

Community: this refers to everyone within the project area as a whole. The purpose of this level is to extend the analysis beyond the family to society at large. Communities are complex, however, and usually comprise a number of different groups of people with different interests. So, if a clearly defined 'community' is not meaningful in the context of the project, this level of analysis may be eliminated.

Categories of analysis

Labour: this refers to changes in tasks, level of skills (skilled, unskilled, formal education, training), and labour capacity (how many people and how much they can do).

Time: this refers to changes in the amount of time (in hours, days, etc.) it takes to carry out the tasks associated with the activity.

Resources: this refers to changes in access to capital, resources, etc.
Cultural factors: this refers to changes in social aspects of the participants' lives (changes in gender role or status, for example) as a result of the project.

The recommended method of completing the GAM is for the target group to work first in small groups, and then for the groups to come together to share their analyses. If the GAM is used at the design or planning stage, they should address questions about the potential impact of the project or programme on labour, time, resources, and cultural factors and status, in each case for women and girls, and men and boys separately. This process will allow participants the opportunity to raise further questions, obtain more information, suggest modifications to the design, and to accept or decline to participate. If the GAM is used at the implementation or monitoring phase, the questions should be directed at changes experienced according to each of these levels and categories, with unexpected results noted and addressed. This also allows for the opportunity to re-orient the project or programme to accommodate unexpected changes in circumstances.

Asking questions

When the Matrix has been filled in, the group discusses a number of questions:

1. Are the effects listed above desirable? Are they consistent with project or programme goals?
2. How will this activity affect those who do not participate?
3. Unexpected results – to be identified during implementation.

The group then marks with a plus sign (+) if the outcomes are consistent with the project or programme goals, or a minus sign (-) if they are not consistent with the goals. They place a question mark (?) against any outcome that they are not sure about. These are *not* intended to be added up, but merely to give an overview of the different effects of the project or programme. The Matrix should record the *changes*, not the situation itself.

Rani Parker suggests that the categories of the Matrix can be modified to suit particular circumstances, either by sub-dividing or leaving out a category. So, for example, labour can be sub-divided into domestic labour, wage labour, own business, and unpaid (social) labour. If a category is not relevant or measurable, for example impact on the community, it can be omitted. She also suggests that additional levels or categories of analysis can be added, such as age, class, or ethnic group, but warns that no more than two should be added as it will make the Matrix too unwieldy. So, race and gender, or class and gender, would be suitable dimensions of a GAM in certain settings; all three might be possible in some contexts. Community could also be subdivided into high income and low income, or into various ethnic groups.

Application to educational settings

In an educational context, there are a number of possible uses for the Matrix if it is modified. Some examples might be designing, or assessing the impact of
- a management structure in a school or college;
- an equal opportunity policy, or staff-development policy;
- a student council or a parent-teacher association;
- a training or literacy programme
- a programme to change attitudes towards sex and gender among female and male students.

In such cases, the Matrix could be modified so that the vertical column reads:

| Female students |
| Male students |

and/or:

| Female staff |
| Male staff |

These categories might be subdivided into teaching and non-teaching staff. The horizontal column could be modified to read:

| Activities | Time | Skills | Resources | Outputs | Social/educational impact |

Case study 1: women's silk-reeling project[9]

A modified Matrix was used effectively in a research study to measure the impact of training provided by NGOs in four countries on women's small businesses. It was therefore being used as an evaluation tool by the researcher and did not follow the participatory mode advocated by Rani Parker. However, as it involved the researcher in extensive interviewing and conversation with the women as they went about their work, it did try to present their views and perspectives in the same way as a participatory workshop might. If the Matrix had been used in a project framework (planning, implementation, or evaluation) rather than as part of a research study, a participatory mode could have been used effectively.

The training provided by the projects was either in business skills, such as basic book keeping, or in technical skills, such as food processing, combined with some gender-awareness raising. The Matrix was modified so as to encapsulate the key measurements (indicators), that is, that the newly acquired or enhanced skills would lead to changes in types of activity; that the allocation of time to these activities, the resources required, and the outputs (income), would lead ultimately to changes in the women's status. The Matrix used was as follows:

	Activities	Time	Skills	Resources	Economic Outputs	Social Impact
Women						
Men						
Household						

This case study reports the findings of only one of the four projects. This was a project run by an Indian NGO in the late 1990s working with scheduled-caste women engaged in silk reeling. Its overall aim was to empower some of the poorest and most disadvantaged women in Indian society by transforming them from poorly paid labourers engaged in reeling silk into successful independent entrepreneurs. These women's families were heavily indebted, many of their men-folk did not have regular employment since they believed that it was beneath their dignity to work for anyone else in the village, and the women's reeling work was also seasonal and uncertain. For most families, if the women did not work, they did not eat. The project would provide an existing women's savings and thrift group with assistance to set up their own small silk-reeling businesses and to carry out all the business aspects themselves such as buying the raw material (cocoons) and selling the spun silk. It was hoped that the women would earn three or four times their current income. This was a particularly ambitious project in an industry dominated by male entrepreneurs.

The project inputs consisted of intensive training over five weeks, small loans to each woman for the purchase of a reeling unit and subsequent working capital, and follow-up support. The training aimed at developing their skills and confidence in managing all aspects of silk reeling, teaching them basic book keeping, and encouraging group solidarity. Given male domination in all aspects of Indian society, with women's limited involvement in decision making, restricted interaction with men outside the family, and lack of mobility, the NGO running the project wisely consulted the women's men-folk about their involvement and explained the project's aims. All the men expressed their support and gave permission for their wives to be involved. Ten women were selected for training. They were to act as role models to other women in the community, who would participate at a later stage.

The NGO provided a male escort who accompanied the women to the local cocoon market and to the silk exchange. This was intended to help them gain confidence in their ability to become independent entrepreneurs, to control and manage their business, and to participate effectively in buying and selling. The system initiated was a five-day cycle, during which two women would take it in turns to buy cocoons for the whole group in the local market. These would then be distributed to the group, the women would reel the silk individually over three days, then pool it, and another two women would take it to the regional Silk Exchange to sell. The income would be used to pay off the loan to the NGO, just keeping enough to buy a new batch of cocoons, and to pay for the necessary labour and fuel. The project was ambitious and sought to empower the women in a very real sense. The NGO insisted that the reeling licence be in the woman's name (and hence the unit belonged to her), that the purchase of cocoons as well as the sale of silk be carried out by the women, and that the loans were made available only to them. Male involvement was limited to helping out in the reeling unit or engaging in marginal tasks such as buying husk for fuel. In effect, the project was proposing a daring role reversal, the women becoming the owners of the business, the husbands in some cases the employees.

In order to measure the impact that the training had on the women, it was necessary to separate out the training input from the other inputs (loan and support). The researcher conducted a baseline survey of each woman just before the first training started, and then visited each woman in turn every two months over a ten-month period. She then returned three years later to see what impact the project had had on their lives over the longer term. After each visit, she completed a Matrix for each woman, and then consolidated these. Table 6.1 outlines what the first of the consolidated Matrices showed.

Questions

Are the effects listed above desirable? Are they consistent with project goals?
Yes, very positive effects for women in terms of much increased status, motivation, confidence, etc. and a small increase in income.

How does this activity affect those who do not participate?
Other women will join the scheme later; some changes to husband's lives (see below); greater share of domestic work falls on children and other female relatives.

Are there any unexpected results?
There has been no change in decision making in the household, a very small profit only, and conflict is starting to emerge among the women over sharing out the cocoons. They are resentful at the time spent in meetings and some try to excuse themselves when it is their turn to go to the Silk Exchange. Their husbands complain about having to accompany them to the bus stop in the next village in the middle of the night when it is their turn to go to sell the silk, and then meet them when they return the following evening.

Table 6.1 Modified GAM to monitor impact of silk reeling project

	Activities	Time	Skills	Resources	Economic outputs	Social impact
Women	+ Productive activity as own business + Livestock rearing as before + Increased group activities	+ Increase in working days + Coping with domestic & productive work − Unit closes on days when they go to the market − Takes time to divide up cocoons in the group − Tired, not enough time to do domestic work or eat properly	+ Bidding for cocoons + Selling the silk + Awareness of business aspects + Assessing quality of cocoons and silk + Oral calculations + Handling large amounts of money + Group decision making	+ Licence in woman's name + Manual labour and marketing skill + Money to buy fuel and cocoons + Can hire labour	+ Slight increase in income + Increased savings − Debt to NGO	+ Change in status from wage earner to entrepreneur + Mobility, boldness, more communication with others + Conscious of time and money + Sense of security (more work) + Motivation + Self respect, peace of mind + Perceived respect from others + Better food (meat) & can buy foodstuffs more cheaply in bulk − Decision making in household remains the same − Some conflict over sharing of cocoons, time spent on meetings, quality of silk
Men	+ Now work in family unit when idle before − Escort women to bus stop at night	− Accompanying women to the bus stop and waiting long hours for their return	+ Some reeling and other skilled tasks + Calculates profit and loss for women	+ Physical labour	+ Some savings on wages of a reeler / turner	+ Supportive of women's activities − Unhappy about escorting women − Becoming resentful − Uneasy at women's 'boldness'
Household	− Girls' domestic work increases − and + child labour increases, but in the home rather than outside					+ Children are happy – more money in home − Other women in household have to do more domestic work

78 | *Practising Gender Analysis in Education*

By the time of the next visit two months later, the situation was much less positive. The completed Matrix showed that on the positive side

- the women continued to improve their skills in doing business: in bidding in the market, assessing the quality of cocoons, oral calculations, etc.
- They were still confident that their activities would become profitable.
- They felt their status in the community had increased.

However, on the negative side

- the expected increase in income had not materialised.
- The price of silk had dropped, and they were reluctant to sell at a loss. Until they sold more, they could not get more loans from the NGO.
- Resentment was growing among the women towards the NGO, which had persuaded them to join the scheme.
- Their husbands also felt resentful at being excluded from the project; they saw no benefits from the scheme and tried to cause trouble between the women by interfering.
- Several husbands used violence against their wives.
- Some women became fatalistic.
- They could no longer find work as agricultural labourers as nobody wanted to employ them (for fear that they would leave as soon as their business picked up again).
- They could no longer borrow money: the entrepreneurs who engaged them before used to give them loans; they now had to beg relatives for help.

A further visit recorded deepening depression and despair, as it was the lean season for cocoons, and the women made very little silk. Their debts mounted and their men-folk became furious at what they now saw as the women's folly in thinking that they could be successful in business. A compromise was finally reached after about eight months, with the NGO allowing the men to become involved in the project and the women to operate on an individual basis. This meant that the men took over the traditional male functions of buying the cocoons and selling the silk. The women were still required to collect the loans from the NGO; otherwise they had reverted more or less to their original role as silk reelers and turners. The women confessed to being relieved, as they had never enjoyed going to the marketplace and mixing with strange men. For a short while, their incomes improved, tension in the household decreased, and the women felt proud of their achievements. But three years on, in 2001, the researcher visited the village and found that the project had died away completely. There was almost no change to the women's lives; indeed, their level of debt as a result of this 'experiment' was higher than before. The only gains appeared to be that they remained somewhat bolder in talking to strangers and moving around on their own.

They were also very keen to see their children educated so that they would not face the world as illiterates, as they themselves had done.

It can be seen that several factors recorded in the first Matrix had become very serious problems by the time the second one was completed: the women were making a loss, conflict was growing in the group, and their male relatives were becoming hostile. If the Matrix exercise had been done by the project team in collaboration with the women and men, these problems might have been tackled as they emerged, rather than being allowed to fester. It would have shown that the men were beginning to sabotage the project, that the women had a poor understanding of costs and profit despite their training in business skills, that conflict was emerging within the group, and that male dealers were colluding against the women so that they did not get the best prices for their silk.

In educational and training terms, the project did not give sufficient importance to raising awareness about gender relations, among the men as well as the women. It concentrated on developing business skills among the women, using trainers who were experts in the silk industry but not in gender relations. The women themselves acknowledged with hindsight that the men also needed gender training. Moreover, the assumption that the women could operate effectively in a market dominated by men was extremely naïve. A step-by-step approach would have been better, involving women gradually in different aspects of silk marketing, working alongside men if appropriate, and combining this with ongoing training in gender awareness, assertiveness, and confidence building. A long-term supportive approach was required, with staging posts to review progress and needs.

With hindsight, it could be seen that the project was too ambitious in its expectation of turning the women into successful entrepreneurs in a notoriously volatile and male-dominated industry. It set the women in positions of unnecessary confrontation with their male relatives by not allowing the men a role in the project, nor a vested interest in its success. There was no attempt by the project managers to develop the men's understanding of what was being attempted, nor to sustain positive relations or regular contact with them. Above all, as problems arose there was no opportunity for raising awareness around gender issues or for examining gender relations among either the men or the women.

Case study 2: the Reflect programme in Malawi

As has been suggested above, the GAM is a very suitable tool for monitoring projects and programmes for their impact on gender relations. This second case study is taken from ActionAid's *Reflect* programme in Malawi.

The information for this case study is taken from the *Reflect* Pilot Project End Evaluation (2001).[10] This reports on the general differences that *Reflect* has made to the literacy circles: action points taken up, changes in participants' lives, and benefits experienced. The numbers of female and male participants is not given, but it is stated that overall there was a predominance of women. Box 2 shows the reported findings.

Although information has been gathered and summarised on the participants' use of their newly acquired skills and knowledge, most of this is not recorded according to gender. Many of the activities seem to be traditional female tasks. In particular, the language contained in a list of 'other changes that have occurred in their lives' suggests that it is only women who have experienced changes. These are:

- They can participate in development activities and can solve community problems.
- They have taken up leading positions in various local structures, e.g. Committee member of the VMC, chairlady of the irrigation committee and treasurer for the irrigation scheme, Vice-chair and secretary of the circle committee.
- They can read letters and know the difference between different days of the week.
- They can run small businesses.
- They are no longer shy and can mix with others.

Yet, the evaluation does report male views from some groups. Important questions that could be raised are:

- If men were also participants, which of the above activities were they engaged in, what new skills did they acquire, and did this change their lives?
- If they shared more of the tasks, did the family benefit and, if so, in what way?

If the GAM was used at the design stage in a participatory mode, it would be possible to set up a monitoring mechanism to record activities, time, skills, resources, economic outputs, and impact on status as a result of the literacy classes. This could be done separately for women, men, their children, and the community (or whichever categories of analysis were considered appropriate). It would then be able to assess the extent to which the *Reflect* programme really had met female and male needs and interests, which women and men had benefited most, and how their lives had changed for the better. Sara Longwe's Women's Empowerment Framework could also have been used in this setting. This would have allowed an indication of whether it was women or men who used these newly acquired skills, and the level of empowerment. This could then have led to a discussion of the gender-specific nature of some of these activities, for example: Who takes the children to hospital? Whose responsibility is family hygiene? Who cleans the area round the borehole? Who attends meetings, and who contributes to the discussion? Do women argue with traders about change, or only men? Why are some tasks

Box 2 Findings from *Reflect* literacy circles, Malawi

Clinic / Hospital: They can read the names of their children and also the weight of the children on the clinic cards. They are able to detect whether the weight increases or decreases. They know how to take care of their children and how to give the correct dosage of medicine. If the medicine does not help they are able to take the child to hospital and would know if the doctor gives them the same medicine again and they are able to question him about it. They can read notices and signs at the hospital that tell them to which room they should go. They have learnt about various health topics in the circle: hygiene and sanitation, environmental cleanliness, etc. They take care of their children in a hygienic way.

Gardens: They know how to apply fertiliser and are able to read the names and types of maize seeds and fertiliser. More people are growing vegetables and use good agricultural practices. They use manure and their harvest has improved. They know how to space when growing crops and to weed early. They make ridges and plant vertical grass so that soil is preserved. They practice crop rotation.

Church: They are able to read from the Bible and sing from the hymnbook, they can also find the right place in these books. Participants have also taken up positions in church: Sunday-school teacher, chairperson and treasurer of women's groups, song leader, etc.

Grinding Mill: They are able to work out the costs of the amount they want to grind and also how much change they should get.

Well / borehole: They clean the surrounding area at the well / borehole and have learnt healthy sanitation practices. When they use risky water they boil it first.

Forest: They have stopped cutting down trees carelessly and they also grow fruit trees. They know which trees add nutrients to the soil and preserve those trees.

Meetings: They prepare before they go to meetings and they can learn from other people in the meetings, but they are also able to participate because of the exposure they had in the circles. They can vote by writing instead of using their thumbs. They can take minutes and write down action plans.

Wedding ceremonies: Can read the invitations.

Funerals: Can write the names of people that come with condolences.

Market: They can work with money and change. They can recognise the different shops and can buy the right quantity of a product, e.g. 2 kg. They are able to question the seller if they receive less. They have learnt to look for quality products and not only quantity. They can read prices of different items.

Home: They clean utensils well when preparing food. They practice family planning. When they want to sell a domestic animal they know to charge the right price. Women are able to confront their husbands about household finances. They can read letters when they receive it. When constructing houses they know the right amount of bricks to use.

School: They are able to check the progress of their children at school and can know when a child is failing. They realise the importance of sending their children to school.

Table 6.2 A GAM to measure the impact of the *Reflect* literacy programme

Skills (literacy, numeracy, etc.)	Activities	Time	Outputs	Social impact
Can read basic text	Read child's weight at hospital, notices, invitations to weddings, hymns at church, instructions on medicine bottles, fertilizer, seed packets	Save time seeking literate neighbour to read for them		Greater self-esteem
Can write names	Record those who come with condolences			
Can do basic calculation on paper			Work out costs	Greater self-esteem, not so easily cheated
Can vote with name rather than thumb print			Attend public meetings	Greater self-esteem
Awareness	Of health and hygiene environment		Stop cutting trees down, clean borehole	Community collaboration

carried out only by women and others by men? What does 'They practise family planning' mean? Finding answers to these questions might facilitate real change.

The GAM could also be used effectively with the Oxfam Primary Education Project in Tanzania (chapter 5) at both the design and monitoring stages.

Commentary

Uses

The GAM is a participatory tool, which can be used at different stages of the project cycle to analyse and monitor changes in gender relations. In its original form it uses a participatory methodology, working closely with communities over a period of time. It can be transformatory, in that it raises awareness of gender (and other) issues as it monitors. It therefore operates at both the practical and the strategic levels simultaneously. As has been seen in the Indian case above, it can also be used for research and impact assessment.

The Matrix, as described in Rani Parker's training manual, is easy and practical to follow. It is flexible, allowing for changes or additions to levels and categories of analysis. The Matrix is designed for those working at the grassroots with communities. The methodology is straightforward and does not require additional resources.

Recording reality and complexity: It allows for the collection of complex and in-depth data, and for the itemisation of tasks and inputs, and so allows less scope for generalised assertions about empowerment by distinguishing rhetoric from reality (as reported in chapter 1). The GAM facilitates the expression and recording of diversity, and discourages generalisation and simplification, which some other gender analysis frameworks might encourage.

A dynamic tool: It monitors changes over time, including those that are unexpected, and is therefore a dynamic tool. It allows for the identification of problems or resistance during the course of the project, and therefore offers a troubleshooting function and the opportunity to address problems before it is too late.

Integrated gender approach: It examines the impact on men as well as women, and on the household and the community. It therefore examines gender issues both as they relate to the individual, to the couple, and to the family and community. It is an integrated approach, resisting the tendency to view women and men as separate groups. It does not focus exclusively on women. The GAM could be used with men or other social groups as the target of the project.

Limitations

The GAM needs a good facilitator. A trained or experienced person may not be available within the community, and an outsider would have to be found. It is less suited to monitoring change in organisational settings because of the complexity of the Matrix.

It is repetitive. Filling in the matrix can be time-consuming, and it is necessary to repeat it several times. It is also a rather complicated process. Sometimes it is not easy to separate out and measure changes that have occurred since the previous visit, from changes since the start of the project.

Addressing problems: Once negative aspects of change have been identified, they must be addressed, so it is highly undesirable to stop completing the Matrix before the end of the project. It can produce misleading outcomes if certain problems are not addressed at an early stage. Some community members may be reluctant to discuss certain problems and negative impacts freely, perhaps for fear that funding will cease.

Use with communities: It assumes that all members of the community have a voice. As with the PRA approach generally, those who are marginalised or discriminated against may be silenced by the process. Some women too may find it difficult to express their sentiments and fears in front of others.

It assumes that communities are basically consensual and can agree on priorities, procedures, etc. As John Pryor points out in his study of understandings of education in a Ghanaian village (2002), much development work is based on a misplaced, over-romanticised view of community.

The GAM does not look beyond the community, it cannot foresee or influence outside forces, such as market changes or government policy. This exposes the community to the risk of failure because of unforeseen circumstances.

Further reading

Parker, A. Rani (1993) *Another Point of View: a Manual on Gender Analysis Training for Grassroots Workers*, New York: UNIFEM.
This is a well-designed training manual with step-by-step instructions. It is also available from Women Ink, New York.

7 | The Social Relations Approach

Introduction

The Social Relations Approach to gender and development planning was developed during the early 1990s by Naila Kabeer at the Institute of Development Studies (IDS) at the University of Sussex, UK. It is firmly grounded in structural feminist thinking, which focuses on the interchange between social relations and patriarchy (Weedon 1997). In the context of education, there are parallels with the structuralist accounts of schooling of Bourdieu and Bernstein, where social identities are formed through a process of internalisation of three core classifications: those of age, sex, and social class (see Arnot 2002, chapter 4). The same social relations classifications are to be found in the family and the workplace. It differs from the other frameworks in that it engages in an analysis of institutional *relations* rather than focusing on roles, resources, and activities (as in the Harvard Framework and the Gender Analysis Matrix). It takes the four key institutions of society to be the State, the market, the community, and the family or kinship. It encourages analysis between these institutions as well as within a single institution. As with the other frameworks, Naila Kabeer's approach provides a structure for planning an intervention based on the gender analysis that has been undertaken. It is complicated to apply to practical situations, however, and should be undertaken only when there is sufficient time to engage thoroughly with the concepts around which it is constructed.

The approach is fully explained in Naila Kabeer's book *Reversed Realities: Gender Hierarchies in Development Thought* (1994) and in a paper by Naila Kabeer and Ramya Subrahmanian (1996) 'Institutions, Relations and Outcomes: Framework and Tools for Gender-aware Planning'. The summary below draws heavily on the account provided in *A Guide to Gender-Analysis Frameworks*.

Basic principles

This approach is intended as a method of analysing the gender inequalities within institutionalised relations that affect the distribution of resources, responsibilities, and power. It can also serve as an aid for designing policies and programmes that support women as agents of their own development. It is a powerful vehicle for examining and explaining the institutional construction and maintenance of gender relations. It concentrates on the relationships between people and their relationship to resources and activities, and the way in which these are re-worked through institutions such as the State or the market.

The Social Relations Approach can be used in a narrow application to analyse how gender inequality is formed and reproduced within a single institution. Alternatively, it can be applied more broadly to reveal how gender and other inequalities are interlinked through interaction between different institutions, creating situations which disadvantage certain individuals and groups in multiple ways. Naila Kabeer makes the point that there are efforts to move beyond the task of integrating gender issues into mainstream development, to the more challenging task of transforming the meaning of development from a gender perspective. Transforming development practice (rather than just 'adding women on') requires a focus on the nature of institutional rules and practices and the way in which they embody male agency, needs, and interests. This implies offering different bases for claiming resources (including both biological difference and socially constructed disadvantage) with differing degrees of transformatory potential (Kabeer 1996: 15–16). We have to recognise that men and women are different, and that between women and between men there are also differences. Therefore, if our goal is social justice rather than formal equality, then the 'how' of a policy or plan is as important as the 'what'.

Social relations

Naila Kabeer uses the term 'social relations' to describe the structural relationships that create and reproduce systemic differences in the positioning of groups of people. Such relationships largely determine our identity, what our roles and responsibilities are, and what claims we can make. They determine our rights and the control that we have over our own lives and those of others. Social relations produce inequalities, which ascribe to each individual a position in the structure and hierarchy of their society. Gender is one type of inequality generated by social relations; others are class, race, ethnicity, caste, kinship, age, and (dis)ability.

Social relations are dynamic and changing; they are not fixed or immutable. Changes in government policy, labour-market legislation, economic trends, and so on can all have an impact on social relations. Human action, such as a public protest, mass campaign, or civil uprising, can also change social relations. Social relations determine what tangible and intangible resources are available to groups and individuals, and what social networks they have access to. Poverty arises out of people's unequal social relations, which dictate unequal access to resources, benefits, claims, and responsibilities. Poor women in particular are denied access to formal resources, so that they have to rely on other forms of social capital such as networks of family, friends, or interest groups, or patronage and dependency, as a critical part of their survival strategy. The role of education is in part to provide young people with the knowledge, information, and skills to help them to reduce their dependency on others and to challenge inequitable social relations.

Institutional analysis

Naila Kabeer defines an institution as a framework of rules for achieving certain social or economic goals (Kabeer 1996: 17). Institutions produce, reinforce, and reproduce social relations, thereby creating and perpetuating social difference and inequality. She suggests four key institutional locations: the State, the market, the community, and family and kinship. In an era of globalisation and international consortia and alliances, the international community can also be considered as an institution. These institutions are not ideologically neutral, and they are not independent of each other: a change in the policy or practice of one institution may bring about change in the others. For example, changes in the labour market which allow many more women to obtain paid employment are likely to bring about changes to relationships within the family and the community. Expansion of secondary or higher education will increase the supply of skilled labour, which may dampen salary levels and increase unemployment; this may also have an effect on the family and on women's access to jobs.

In contrast to 'institution', the term 'organisation' refers to the specific structural forms that institutions take. In the current context, schools are organisations; they are part of the educational system, which is an important arm of the State (an institution). In engaging in gender analysis we need to examine the way in which institutions create and reproduce inequalities through their organisations. Gender inequalities are not confined purely to household and family relationships but are reproduced across all four institutions. Bringing about institutional change requires negotiation, bargaining, and reciprocity at all levels and in all domains.

In the educational context, in almost all countries it is schools, colleges, and universities that are the principal organisations by which the State reproduces its ideology among the young. While the State jealously guards its power to determine the structures of schooling (including varying degrees of control over curriculum content, teacher training, assessment, etc.) and hence control over its capacity for social reproduction, it is not the only provider of formal education. The market is also involved in the buying and selling of education through private provision, as is to a lesser degree both the community (through schools run by community-based organisations and NGOs) and the family (where parents choose to educate their children at home). Private and community provision has grown largely because the State is unable to meet public demand for schooling, especially in poor countries, and because the quality of the education that it provides is seen as unsatisfactory. Privatisation and competition are also part of the capitalist state ideology, and so are considered just as applicable to basic services such as education and health as to other sectors such as industry or commerce.

It is not surprising that education has a powerful role to play in the perpetuation of state ideology. Schools play an important part in contributing to individual achievement, social and economic progress, and democratic practices. However, as Nelly Stromquist (1998: 397) points out:

> ... *they are powerful ideological institutions*[11] *that transmit dominant values, and function as mechanisms of social control. Schools transmit values that not only reproduce social class but also maintain gender structures. The formal school system contributes to the reproduction of gender inequalities through such mechanisms as selective access to schooling, the content of what is being taught and what is not and how it is taught, and the kinds of knowledge men and women (and boys and girls) get. School curriculum functions to legitimate the political order, and any curriculum change often involves changing the definition of knowledge held by dominant groups; thus these changes are often fiercely contested.*

On the gendered nature of institutions, Naila Kabeer (1996: 17–18) writes: 'Many of the official ideologies through which institutions describe themselves tend to get uncritically reproduced in social science text books, in public policy and in popular discourse, while the compartmentalised nature of the social sciences has led to the treatment of key institutions as somehow separate and distinct from each other, the subject matter of different disciplines'.

Kabeer argues that to understand how social difference and inequalities are produced and reproduced through institutions, it is necessary to move beyond the official ideology of bureaucratic neutrality to examine the actual rules and practices of institutions to uncover their core values and assumptions. Her suggested institutional locations and the types of organisation that they incorporate are usefully outlined in the *A Guide to Gender-Analysis Frameworks* and shown in Table 7.1.

Table 7.1 Four key institutional locations

Social relations: institutional analysis

Key institutional locations	Organisational / structural form
State	Legal, military, administrative organisations
Market	Firms, financial corporations, farming enterprises, multinationals
Community	Village tribunals, voluntary associations, informal networks, patron–client relationships, NGOs
Family / kinship	Household, extended families, lineage groupings, and so on

Source: March *et al.* 1999: 104

Kabeer sees each location as pursuing a dominant or 'official' ideology (which is espoused in much development-policy discourse, but is not necessarily born out in reality):

- The State pursues the national interest and national welfare.
- The market pursues profit maximisation.
- The community, including NGOs, is involved in service provision.
- Family and kinship is about altruism; it is a cooperative, not a divisive institution.

Five aspects of social relations shared by institutions

Although institutions vary in their purpose, their culture, and their working practices, according to Kabeer they share five distinct but inter-related components of social relationships: rules, resources, people, activities, and power. Analysing institutions according to these categories helps us to understand why some people gain and others lose out. This is applicable to education as an institution (part of the State). The five categories are (taken from *A Guide to Gender-Analysis Frameworks*):

Rules: how things get done

Institutional behaviour is governed by rules. These may be official and written down or unofficial and expressed through norms, values, traditions, and customs. In schools and other educational organisations, there is a gendered dimension to rules in terms of who does what, how it is done, and who will benefit.

Resources: what is used, what is produced?

Institutions mobilise and distribute resources; these may be human resources (labour, education, skills, etc.), material resources (food, assets, land, money), or intangible ones (information, political power, goodwill, or contacts). As the Harvard Framework analysis shows, organisations often distribute resources according to social categories (gender, ethnicity, religion, for example) tied to rules.

People: who is in, who is out, who does what?

Institutions are selective about whom they allow in and whom they exclude, who has access to various resources and responsibilities, and who is positioned where in the hierarchy. This selection may reflect class, gender, or other social inequalities. For example, in the UK labour market most managing directors are male, middle class, and white; most workers on the London Underground are male and black; most teachers are female and white. However, there are many more male head teachers, college principals, and professors than there are female, which is indicative of a hierarchy.

Activities: what is done?

Institutions do things: they try to achieve things by following their own rules and ensuring routinised practice for carrying out tasks. These activities can be productive, distributive, or regulative. They consider who does what, and what they get for doing it.

Certain tasks become attached to certain social groups, sometimes in the belief that they are the only people capable of doing them, for example, women as carers of the sick, the young, and the elderly. Rewards (including monetary gain and status) vary, for example, surgeons (mostly men) earn many times more than nurses (mostly women); a head teacher (more likely to be a man) earns more than a teaching assistant (more likely to be a woman). Such a hierarchy of rewards reinforces inequalities between women and men, and between different social classes. People who only carry out a particular task become very good at it, and particular attributes are attached to this group as a result. For example, women's 'nimble fingers' make them more 'suitable' than men for assembly-line work in the electronics industry; it is considered 'natural' that primary school teachers should be women, as this is a job which involves the 'caring' and 'nurturing' responsibilities associated with women.

Power: who decides and whose interests are served?

Institutions embody relations of authority and control. Few institutions are egalitarian even if they profess to be so. The unequal distribution of rules, resources, and activities ensures that some institutional actors have authority and control over others. All educational systems are hierarchical, with the Minister at the top and moving down through ranks of provincial and district officials to head teachers, teachers, and finally pupils, who wield the least power.

An institutional gender analysis of the educational system as a key arm of the State can be carried out using the Social Relations Approach. This can also be applied to a single organisation (e.g. a school or even a classroom), illustrating the way in which the social relations that are framed by educational structures operate at the micro-level. Such analyses illustrate how formal education discriminates on the grounds of gender, race, and/or class at all levels, for example, an examination of how teachers and pupils interact in the classroom will usually reveal stereotypical patterns of behaviour informed by social relations based on gender, class, religion, etc. These structural relationships in education have been researched and written about extensively in industrialised countries (for example, by Bourdieu and Passeron 1977, Young 1971, Weiner 1994). A more challenging analysis would involve examining how the educational system intersects with other sub-components of the State (such as the law, social services, the civil service), or with the community, the family, and the market, to reproduce social inequality.

Naila Kabeer's approach could have been used as an alternative to the Harvard Framework in analysing the teachers' college in Nigeria (chapter 4). There is clearly some overlap between the five categories of analysis listed above and the 'activities' and 'access and control of resources' categories of the Harvard framework. However, Kabeer's categories of 'rules' and 'people' provide a useful additional dimension to the boundaries of what is and is not acceptable (rules) and who is included and who is excluded (people), which is not clearly picked up in the other framework.

The following case study offers an institutional analysis using the Social Relations Approach to school provision of HIV/AIDS education in Uganda.

Case study: HIV/AIDS education in Uganda[12]

This is an analysis across all four institutions (State, market, community, and family or kinship), which seeks to illustrate the shortcomings and difficulties of teaching about HIV/AIDS through the school. It takes Uganda as an example of a country which has experienced a dramatic decline in HIV infection rates over the past decade, in part through energetic and sustained government campaigns. However, the extent to which the school has helped to reduce these infection rates among the young by persuading them to change their sexual practice is not clear. This analysis may clarify its role.

Uganda has been praised for its exemplary and energetic early approach to tackling the epidemic. It is the one African country to have experienced dramatic declines in infection rates; Senegal has also experienced a decline but not as steep as that in Uganda, where it is claimed that rates have fallen from a high of 30 per cent in some parts of the country in 1992 to eight per cent nationally in 2001. The epidemic has clearly peaked in Uganda, with the decline being most noticeable in the 15–29 age group. This appears to be the result of an aggressive public health campaign with support and encouragement from the President of Uganda. The early fear-based messages about AIDS ('AIDS kills') have been replaced by messages that stress compassion, solidarity, and hope, and which aim to reduce the stigma attached to AIDS so that individuals feel that they can tell family members and sexual partners about their status. These messages also promote abstinence, faithfulness in sexual relationships, and the use of condoms during sexual intercourse.

Early surveys in the 1990s showed that young Ugandans become sexually active at an early age, often as young as 13 or 14 years (Hyde *et al.* 2001: 12). This clearly exposes many young people to a high risk of HIV infection. Girls are the most vulnerable, given that in the high-prevalence countries they are six times more likely to be infected than boys (Mirembe and Davies 2001: 402). However, the sustained campaign by the Ugandan government to change sexual behaviour appears to have had an impact on this younger age group, with a 1997 study showing that growing numbers are having sex at a later age (a two-year delay), and those who are sexually active adopting condom-use faster than other sections of the population. A claim is therefore made that 'education reduces the likelihood of being HIV positive' (Hyde *et al.* 2001: 17).

While this record is impressive, the way in which education has contributed to the decline needs to be scrutinised. Relevant questions that need answering include:

- Have schools played a central part in helping to change sexual behaviour among adolescents, or have the education messages come from other sources?
- Is it education alone that has reduced sexual activity, or are there other factors?
- Does a change in sexual behaviour (fewer partners, greater use of condoms) include a change in the gendered nature of sexual relationships, and in particular greater female control over when and how sex takes place? And if so, how sustainable is this, given the dominant pattern of power imbalance in gender relations across all social institutions?
- These same studies show that sexual behaviour in those over the age of 30 has not changed despite the public campaigns. Is it possible that schools, which it is claimed reproduce and maintain social structures and relations, have been able to spearhead changes not experienced more widely in society?

In fact, the Rockefeller study into HIV/AIDS and schooling in three African countries on which this case study is based, found that most work with adolescents was the result of community initiatives, public campaigns, and media exposure. Relatively little had been done by schools themselves, even though some outside agencies were operating within schools and were providing training to female and male teachers in health-education strategies, guidance, and counselling. Overall, however, the authors found that

- there was very little reference to HIV/AIDS in the formal curriculum;
- schools depended on invited guests, outreach workers, public campaigns, and counselling from senior male and female teachers to provide AIDS education to students;
- guidance and counselling was an underdeveloped part of the curriculum;
- HIV/AIDS was not seen as a major problem among students.

They concluded that 'although community-based HIV prevention programmes have achieved significant results, the opportunity to make a lasting impression on children during their school years – before they become sexually active – has not been fully utilized' (*ibid*.: 1).

If it is the case that schools have played only a limited role in changing sexual behaviour among adolescents in Uganda, the Social Relations Approach may allow us to unpack some of the reasons for this, and suggest ways in which their involvement can be strengthened. Naila Kabeer suggests analysing the causes and effects of a particular situation according to its immediate, underlying, and structural factors; in this way it is possible to isolate the key factors and to address them through a planned intervention. The following analysis examines the causes and effects of the limited impact of schools on HIV/AIDS prevention, looking at contributory factors across all four institutional locations. Education is taken as representative of the State in this example. Table 7.2 lists aspects of the school, market, community, and household or family that inter-relate and contribute to this limited impact of HIV prevention messages through the school. Table 7.3 sketches out a strategy to strengthen the school's role in the HIV prevention campaign. The lower section of the Table 7.2 identifies factors that contribute to the core problem, the upper section the consequences of these factors. Table 7.3 lists the means to address the problem and the anticipated ends (outcomes). It is probably easiest to understand the tables by looking at the causes and effects by level (immediate causes and immediate effects, intermediate causes and effects, etc.).

This inter-institutional analysis reveals a wide range of factors, some originating from within schools and some from other social institutions, which contribute to the limited impact of schools in passing on health messages about safe sex. The analysis shows schools to be highly gendered places, where unequal power relations are played out and gendered identities are developed and reproduced.

This scenario conflicts with the Ugandan government's current message as one that seeks to empower individual actors to take responsibility for their own actions and thus avoid getting the HIV virus (Hyde *et al.* 2001: 23).

Table 7.2 Inter-institutional analysis of reasons for limited involvement of the school in HIV prevention

Long term effects: continuing neglect of women's and children's rights

Continuing gender inequality, with few women in decision-making positions and women in lower paid and less skilled jobs than men

Intermediate effects: decline in HIV/AIDS infection rates may slow down

Gender bias and gender violence in social relations in and outside school are sustained

School continues to promote dominant views of masculinity and femininity

Erosion of family life due to AIDS-related bereavement

Immediate effects: limited effective teaching about HIV/AIDS either in the school or in the home / community

Teaching style raises awareness and fear of HIV/AIDS but does not bring about change in gender relations

Continuing denial that school children engage in sexual activity, which places them at risk

Adolescents, especially girls, continue to be exposed to sexual aggression and to engage in transactional sex

The core problem: schools' limited impact on HIV/AIDS prevention

Immediate causes

School: reluctance to teach sex education / HIV prevention in school in an open way

Lack of appropriate training for teachers

Reluctance to admit that young children engage in sexual activity, while teaching abstinence as the solution to the HIV epidemic

Reluctance to acknowledge girls' vulnerability to sexual violence

Acceptance that male teachers have affairs with schoolgirls

Authoritarian / didactic teaching style and superficial learning, which does not promote behaviour-change

School as a site for promoting dominant views of appropriate male and female behaviour, which encourages violence against girls

Market: limited income opportunities for girls, which oblige them to accept gifts from male students, teachers, and 'sugar daddies'

Community: difficulty in providing for orphans

Difficulty in talking about sex openly, limited sex education for children, especially with the decline of traditional initiation

Transactional sex between older men ('sugar daddies') and schoolgirls

Myth that having sex with a virgin cures AIDS

Family: girls stay at home to nurse the sick and undertake additional tasks, and so miss school

Early marriage

Table 7.2 Inter-institutional analysis of reasons for limited involvement of the school in HIV prevention *continued*

Intermediate causes

School: the imposition of school fees at secondary level through structural adjustment programmes forces some girls into transactional sex, or to drop out of school

Inadequate support for bereaved families and orphans, making the latter vulnerable to sexual exploitation

Failure to address the sexual harassment of female teachers / students by male teachers / students and to punish inappropriate gendered behaviour

Media messages promoting equality in gender relations which conflict with the reality of a male-dominated school culture

Culture of masculinity, which encourages boys to engage in risk-taking behaviour, so as to prove themselves, and to appear 'tough'; high levels of bullying by male students

Peer pressure to conform to gendered behaviour styles

Market: girls and women seen as a 'commodity' to be bought, with men ready to pay for sex

Sexual harassment in the workplace

Male migration to urban areas in search of work encourages multiple sexual partners

Discriminatory employment practices, with well paid jobs held primarily by men

Community: dominant male roles in the community – women mostly in community maintenance, not political roles

Conservative views of gender – power of opinion leaders (religious, political, etc.)

Beliefs around male virility and prowess – men must have children (and so need unprotected sex)

Male sexual promiscuity is condoned while emphasising female virginity / faithfulness; young boys are encouraged to experiment

Health campaigns promote gender-unaware messages about abstinence and safe sex, without acknowledging power differences in sexual relationships

Family: enforcement of social and cultural norms, including early marriage and marriage of widows to a male relative (who may pass on the infection if her husband died of AIDS)

Extended family already eroded by employment practices and labour-market trends; exploitation of orphans

Women unable to negotiate sex and insist on safe sexual practice (e.g. use of condoms with partners); promoting safe sex within marriage questions faithfulness, openness, and truthfulness

Male migration to urban areas in search of work encourages multiple partners

Male dislike of condoms

Less access for women and girls to health facilities than men and boys in poor households

Reliance on women and girls to provide free care and nursing for those sick with AIDS, leading to absenteeism from school.

> **Table 7.2 Inter-institutional analysis of reasons for limited involvement of the school in HIV prevention** *continued*
>
> *Structural causes*
>
> **State:** the gendered structure of society: women treated as inferior to men, as their property, as servicing men; women have fewer legal rights, e.g. ownership of land and property
>
> Reluctance to acknowledge and tackle manifestations of gender inequality such as domestic violence, sex discrimination and sexual harassment in the workplace, sexual harassment and abuse in the school
>
> Power is a male preserve; discourse of incompetence of females; sex is not usually negotiable on equal terms
>
> **Community / Family:** patrilineal society – a marriage contract (bride price) that gives men rights over their wives and children, girls and women have fewer entitlements to ownership of assets (land, etc.) or savings

This message assumes that women have the same opportunities as men to determine when and how sex takes place, which is clearly not the case either for adolescents or for adults. It ignores the role that unequal gender relations and patriarchy play in the spread of the virus and the lack of choice experienced by women in their sexual relationships. This in itself raises questions about the sustainability of any change in sexual behaviour brought about as a result of the campaigns.

As far as adolescents are concerned, it would appear that these campaigns have been relatively successful at transmitting (gender-unaware) messages about HIV/AIDS, passed on by outside facilitators or in some cases specially trained teachers. As a result, school-going children in Uganda, as in many countries in Sub-Saharan Africa, have a high level of knowledge and awareness of the disease. This may deter them from starting sex at an early age and may encourage them to use condoms, but it does not mean that there has been any fundamental change in the nature of the sexual relationships that they form. Hence the question mark over the continuing downward trend of HIV infection rates in Uganda beyond that achieved through the build-up of natural resistance and/or medical intervention; this may not continue unless there is change in the way in which sex is negotiated within relationships, and a change in the male-dominated power structures which sustain all four institutions of social relations. If significant change has only occurred among the young, is this sustainable when the wider social relations remain unchanged?

Intervention

After identifying a problem of gender relations and analysing its causes and effects from a gender perspective, Naila Kabeer proposes the design of an intervention to address the problem by challenging and changing these relations. The next step is therefore to elaborate the range of means and ends that emerge from the close analysis of causes and effects. The gendered effects of the problem provide us with the rationale for a gender-sensitive or gender-redistributive policy response, laying out the immediate needs and longer-term interests which are implicated in it, and sketching out the desired ends which will constitute the overall goals and objectives of the policy response (Kabeer and Subramanian 1996: 35).[13]

Table 7.3 looks at means and ends in relation to a core response (to teach HIV/AIDS effectively in schools). It shows that there are clearly identified strategies for teaching more effectively about HIV/AIDS within schools. There are resource implications to this, but with international agency funding and political will these are not insurmountable. There are also implications in terms of the role that the school can and should play in terms of changing the negatively gendered pattern of relations that develops among adolescents during their school years.

The authors of the Rockefeller report acknowledge that there remain major challenges. AIDS will not be fully defeated until the knowledge gained by young people about HIV/AIDS that has led them to postpone sex or practise safer sex is carried forward into adult life. 'They are ... not yet equipped with the skills to carry these positive behaviours into the long-term formalised relationships (marriage and cohabitation) that are more complex and seem to be unrelated to the decision-making and negotiation skills of their youth that are focused on promoting abstinence. Safer sex within marriage, particularly the use of a condom except when trying to become pregnant with a partner who is known to be HIV negative, brings up issues of trust that few couples are able to confront and resolve' (Hyde *et al.* 2001: 25). And they caution that 'some important gender issues, especially with respect to condom use, faithfulness and openness between spouses, are far from being resolved ... This is particularly an issue for poorly educated women in rural areas. A small number of well educated Kampala women may be able to refuse to have sex with their husbands without condoms, but they are very much in the minority.'(*ibid.*: 26). At the same time, the authors reported that informants felt that government initiatives to address gender gaps, for example in the proportion of female MPs, helped explain what progress had been made, however modest. Although gender relations remain unequal, some women did feel empowered to make sexual decisions and this was contributing to the decline of the infection.

The above analysis shows not only how important are the skills to develop positive social relationships and healthy sexual practices for young people, but also that they are achievable. Schools can do much more to help them to develop constructive relationships and make rational life choices.

Table 7.3 Improving schools' approach to HIV/AIDS prevention

Long-term ends: develop mature citizens who can make independent and informed decisions

Intermediate ends: change school culture and organisation to reflect more equal relationships

Immediate ends: greater awareness and discussion of issues around HIV infection and how to mitigate the impact of the disease
Improved access to information, advice, and counselling
Learning through school-based support system for orphans and infected students and teachers
More constructive and meaningful adolescent relationships

Core response: teach HIV/AIDS effectively in schools

Immediate means: create space for discussion of adolescent issues in a secure environment
Promote communication between teachers and students and between students themselves
Train teachers and outside facilitators to deliver reproductive health messages effectively
Hold open discussions on gender issues, empowerment, relationships; engage in participatory activity (drama, radio, etc.), through extra-curricular and peer-led activity such as AIDS, sports, drama clubs as well as through the curriculum
Give opportunities to students of all ages to voice their concerns and seek information, advice, and counselling on HIV/AIDS, reproductive health and puberty, cultural practices that pose a sexual risk to children and adolescents
Allow condom distribution to school children

Intermediate means: develop a new curriculum with improved HIV/AIDS content, which presents it in a social as well as a medical context
Address the implications of this new curriculum content for assessment, examinations, and inspection
Improve the ability and skills of teachers to teach life skills in a creative and engaging manner, which will enhance understanding of the gendered dimension of sexual relationships and bring about change
Train a cadre of specialist teachers with specific skills in reproductive health education
Develop training materials on HIV/AIDS prevention
Develop and enhance guidance and counselling services; provide students with easy access to information and advice on HIV/AIDS as well as access to HIV testing
Promote the welfare of AIDS orphans and staff living with HIV/AIDS in schools, thus sending messages about how to care for sufferers
Develop partnerships and networks with NGOs and CBOs, the private sector, and other stakeholders in AIDS education

Structural means

Create a gender-sensitive and gender-equitable environment within schools which is hostile to sexual harassment, early sexual activity, and physical violence
Enforce sanctions against those who violate gender rights, e.g. male teachers who threaten female students if they don't have sex with them
Develop a value system in schools that promotes self-esteem and mutual respect, and allows girls in particular to be more assertive and to take on leadership roles.

Commentary

Uses

The Social Relations Approach can be used for many purposes; it is particularly powerful because it is multi-levelled and multi-dimensional. It can be applied to a number of institutions and organisations as well as to a single entity.

Because it engages in institutional analysis, it is useful in helping organisations translate analysis into action, and so it supports efforts at gender mainstreaming. It helps in understanding how structures, processes, and relations inter-relate.

The approach shows how features of one institution link to, reinforce, and influence those of the others, and how inequalities of gender, class, ethnicity, etc. interact and reinforce each other. It shows how changes in one institution, the State, for example, have an impact on other institutions, such as the market. In an educational context, it offers opportunities to clarify links between the gendered aspects of education and jobs, labour legislation, economic forces, and so on.

Strengths

The Approach places gender at the centre of the institutional analysis, where often it is added on; organisations using this analysis are obliged to examine their own practices and address them in their own planning process.

It challenges the myth of the independence and neutrality of institutions and shows that in fact they are inter-related and are social and cultural creations.

It offers both the opportunity for analysis and for identifying strategies for change.

It emphasises the connectedness of men and women and boys and girls through social (gender) relations, while highlighting their different needs and interests.

Limitations

The Social Relations Approach is complicated in practice; it may be difficult to use unless adapted (March *et al.* suggest a modified set of categories: rules, practices, and power).

Conceptually it may be difficult to grasp, for example, the distinction between institutions and between an institution and an organisation are not always clear-cut.

The distinction can be arbitrary between immediate, intermediate, and long-term structural causes and effects, means and ends.

It emphasises structure at the expense of agency; for example, seeing girls as passive victims of 'sugar daddies', when in fact they might choose such relationships to enhance their status within the peer group.

It requires detailed knowledge of the situation being analysed; at the same time it is difficult to use in a participatory way.

It is more appropriate for macro-level analysis (the Harvard Framework, the GAM, and Sara Longwe's Empowerment Framework may all be more appropriate for small case studies).

It ignores other important institutions (e.g. the media, formalised religion) in its analysis of the Social Relations Approach and the examples provided.

Further reading

Arnot, M. (2002) *Reproducing Gender: Essays on Educational Theory and Feminist Politics,* London and New York: RoutledgeFalmer.

Stromquist, N.P. (ed.) (1998) *Women in the Third World: an Encyclopedia of Contemporary Issues,* New York: Garland.

8 | Curriculum-materials analysis

Basic principles

The curriculum, whether in a school, college, or non-formal education or training centre, should never be considered as 'neutral' or 'objective'. It is the product of choices and decisions made by those in charge of selecting what knowledge, information, and skills should be passed on to learners. Certain types of knowledge are considered more important than others depending on the context. So, for example, teaching the speed at which light travels or major events in a nation's history will probably be considered as more important in a school setting than teaching the names of the local football team or the ingredients of a local dish. Which historical 'events' are chosen for highlighting, and from whose perspective they are reported provides additional scope for selectivity and distortion. Likewise, certain skills will be valued more than others. For example, we would expect the ability to do basic mathematical calculations or write a paragraph using complex language to be judged as more important in a school context than learning how to ride a bicycle or catch a fish. School knowledge is almost always defined in very narrow terms as largely abstract and academic. It is usually also viewed in a hierarchical manner, with science and maths traditionally seen as 'high status', 'difficult', and 'objective' subjects, while agriculture and home economics are seen as less important and suitable for the less intelligent. The types of knowledge that should be taught in schools has always been a matter of debate, with some insisting that schools should teach vocationally oriented subjects and others regarding this suggestion with disdain. On balance, however, the desirability and status of school subjects is in large part determined by perceptions of how essential they are for further education and job opportunities.

Inevitably, embedded in the knowledge, information, and skills being passed on are certain values, norms, and biases which reflect the dominant views and beliefs of those who have constructed the curriculum and the learning materials, including what they consider to be important and relevant to learners. Factors such as an all-male curriculum writing team, or the majority of team members belonging to the same ethnic group or living in an urban area, are likely to lead to serious biases. So, examples given in a science textbook might heavily favour interests commonly perceived as 'male' (football, cars, computer games) or urban experiences (traffic lights, roundabouts, and offices). Research shows that learners who have little or no experience or interest in the contexts provided by these examples will be disadvantaged, especially when it comes to testing their knowledge through examinations (Arnot et al. 1998).

Learners' extensive exposure to textbooks and other learning materials through years of schooling serves as a powerful medium for socialising young people into dominant patterns of gender relations and gendered behaviour, which they will carry with them into adult life. When added to this are all the personal biases and preferences of individual teachers, biases in test items in examinations, and the social influences that accompany everyday school experiences (often called 'the hidden curriculum'), the learning environment becomes extremely influential as a socialising force. This is particularly the case with children whose sense of identity is in the process of development and hence vulnerable to individual and societal influence, but it also applies to adults who are following non-formal education programmes of literacy or vocational skills.

Where women are portrayed in a limited range of roles, often dependent on men, and are associated with passive characteristics, such as obedience, loyalty, gratitude, and shyness, this can contribute to a low sense of self-value and low self-esteem, which in turn can lead to under-achievement. If women are portrayed exclusively as wives and mothers, or in low income and unskilled paid work, schoolgirls will not be provided with role models to encourage them to study hard and consider having a career. If men are only portrayed in action-oriented, bravura roles and as characters devoid of weaknesses or emotions, boys will feel that they have to emulate them and that they will be judged as inadequate if they cannot.

To minimise bias, curriculum developers and materials writers need to engage in a systematic analysis and revision of all the materials that are produced for any organised learning activity. It is easy for individuals to think that they are being neutral and balanced in what they write, but time and time again an analysis of materials shows that they are not. As the following case-study material will show, the majority of school textbooks and literacy materials reflect commonly perceived male interests and male preferences in teaching and learning, even in areas where more women are actually engaged, such as is the case with agriculture in Sub-Saharan Africa.

In school, pupils are often required to choose which subjects to study. In some cases, they are allocated to certain subjects according to ability. More often, however, girls are encouraged to go for subjects traditionally seen as 'feminine', such as languages, history, and home economics, and to avoid maths and science, which are seen as the male domain. When science is offered to girls, they may be encouraged to take biology but to leave physics and chemistry for boys. Such choices tend to be seen as 'natural' by both girls and boys because they have come to see the subjects as gender-specific. In turn, these decisions influence life choices and career paths; for example, many opportunities for higher education are cut off if maths is not taken in school leaving examinations.

At the college and university level, the same preferences persist, with female students usually clustered in the arts, humanities, education, and health, while male students dominate in engineering, science, and computer science. Whether these preferences are a product of biology (e.g. different brain structure) or of social conditioning is much debated but there is no doubt that teachers (and parents) play a role in diverting male and female students into certain subject areas seen as appropriate for their sex.

Tools and checklists

A number of tools and checklists exist which can be used when analysing materials for gender bias. Some are rather detailed and complicated but a number are summarised here, and some sample analyses are provided. These tools can be used by curriculum developers and writers of textbooks and other learning materials (such as charts, posters, games, teachers' guides, children's stories, and also newspapers, magazines, and advertisements), and by planners, examination officers, teachers, and teacher trainers. They can also be used by gender trainers and facilitators in awareness-raising workshops. It is important to bear in mind that the gender analysis of textbooks is much more than just counting, for example the number of pictures of female and male characters or appearances in a text, or the number of occupations associated with females or males. This will be a shallow analysis, and little more than tokenism. Only an in-depth analysis of the gendered representations in the text, carried out by individuals who fully grasp and are committed to gender equity considerations, will provide a sound basis for revision.

Sources

Key sources for this section include: P. Brickhill *et al.* (1996) *Textbooks as an Agent of Change: Gender Aspects of Primary School Textbooks in Mozambique, Zambia and Zimbabwe*; Commonwealth Secretariat (1995) *Gender Bias in School Text Books*; W.M. Kabira and M. Masinjila (1997) *ABC of Gender Analysis*; A. Obura (1991) *Changing Images: Portrayal of Girls and Women in Kenyan Textbooks*; M. Sifuniso *et al.* (2000) *Gender-sensitive Editing*; and UNESCO (1997) *Gender Sensitivity: a Training Manual*.

These publications provide much more than a checklist. They offer a framework for extensive analysis and discussion of the ways in which powerful gendered images are transmitted through both text and illustration. Much has been written about the power of written and oral discourse in perpetuating social inequality, including gender inequality (Foucault 1974, Bernstein 1996, Walkerdine 1988). If you intend to engage in gender analysis of texts in a professional capacity (as a curriculum developer, textbook writer, editor, or illustrator), it would be advisable to read around the topic more widely. The ADEA manual on gender-sensitive editing (Sifuniso *et al.* 2000) contains valuable chapters on the principles of design and illustrations, written very much with a professional publishing audience in mind. The Commonwealth Secretariat publication presents a survey of primary textbooks in five Caribbean, 11 African, and three Asian Commonwealth countries. It includes guidelines specifically for textbook writers and producers, and another set for teachers and teacher educators. Brickhill *et al.* (1996) also addresses an audience of publishers and development agencies.

UNESCO: Gender Sensitivity: a Training Manual

As part of its training manual in gender sensitivity, UNESCO has produced a checklist for use with reading materials, based on a workshop on women's self-reliance. This checklist has been designed for use with materials prepared for women's projects. However, it can be used more widely by teachers, literacy facilitators, curriculum developers, and Ministry officials responsible for school-textbook purchases. It is fairly loosely structured, with some questions of a general nature, for example, on the appearance of the booklet (or book). It obviously needs to be adapted for its immediate use, such as if a science textbook is being examined rather than one containing stories.

Guidelines for analysing booklets

1 Summarise the story
2 Does the booklet promote women's self-reliance? What issues are prominent?
   - The multiple roles of women
   - Women taking initiative to control their lives
   - Women questioning their life conditions
   - Women leaders
   - Women as equal partners of men
   - Women in non-traditional employment
3 Is the content realistic?
4 Does the booklet reinforce sex stereotypes? If so, in what way?
5 How are women and men portrayed?
   - As nurturers
   - As economic producers
   - As leaders

6 Can you see any change in the respective roles of women and men in society? In what ways? Discuss whether the same changes will be possible in your own community.

7 Is this booklet easy to read?

8 Are the illustrations attractive and appropriate?

9 Do they portray women and men positively?

10 Is there anything you would like to improve in your booklet?

11 How does this booklet promote the equal partnership between women and men?

12 Do you like the booklet? Discuss your feelings.

Source: UNESCO 1997: 69

Obura: Changing Images

This is a more rigorous and detailed analytical framework, inspired by a UNESCO-sponsored study of Arab, Chinese, Norwegian, and Ukrainian textbooks and a UNESCO study of schoolgirl drop-out in Benin. Anna Obura applied her framework to 24 Kenyan textbooks covering maths, science, technical subjects, languages, and social sciences used through the eight grades of primary school in 1985.[14] Although too detailed for many purposes, it is possible to take a lesson or unit at random in a textbook and apply the analysis. Alternatively, it is possible to analyse one aspect only, for example, the illustrations, or the occupations associated with men and women, or the language of the text. This is particularly useful for those who wish to purchase textbooks or who are reading curriculum materials in draft form. A selective approach also lends itself to gender-awareness training, as the degree of stereotyping is almost always very startling. The examples provided by Anna Obura date from the 1980s; however, most textbooks in Kenya and elsewhere continue to portray the same biases.

Anna Obura carried out her analysis according to the following steps:

1 Qualitative analysis

The whole book was scanned for its visual impact and the flavour of the text.

2 Quantitative analysis

- The number of characters of each sex was counted, each person being counted only once.
- Proper names were listed, categorised as male or female, subdivided into man or woman, boy or girl, and each category counted.
- The number of males and females mentioned were counted, both named and nameless.

- Gender-indicated common nouns were listed (such as mother, fisherman, king) and classified under the categories male or female, adult or child.
- The order of appearance of female and male characters was noted, both in terms of the page and their place on the page and in a sentence.
- The activities and roles of people were listed, categorised, and counted by sex.
- To determine the centrality of the male and female characters, sections of the text were analysed in depth to discover relationships and prominent patterns of presentation.
- Pictures of female and male adults and children were counted in a similar way.

3 Further qualitative analysis

For example, the role models presented for girls contrasted with those for boys; and the method of presenting female characters compared to male characters (order of appearance, whether they are presented as autonomous individuals or only in relationship to males, whether they are accompanied by males or presented as a corollary or complementary to males).

4 An analysis of the language used

For example, an examination of the way in which certain words which denote male association are used as generic or neutral terms (mankind, man, tradesmen, chairman, etc.) and how pronouns are used (e.g. the farmer and his ...).

Anna Obura drew on UNESCO's Ukrainian study for its five categories of analysis:

- frequency and nature of appearance of female characters;
- work/employment roles;
- socio-political roles of males and females;
- the family roles of males and females;
- psychological traits of males and females.

When she applied these categories to the Kenyan textbooks used in her study, she found some startling evidence of gender bias. For example, analysis of the three maths textbooks showed that the presence of females was rare and became increasingly so in the higher classes. Females were presented later in the books than men and were less frequently given a name. Men were portrayed as engaging in a wide range of income generating activities (23 in total), but women in only two (shop keeper and kiosk owner). Pronouns (he/she) were predominantly male. Ownership was largely a male prerogative, with men owning large amounts of land, cattle, vehicles, etc., whereas women had little money and only small businesses (poultry farm, women's cooperative). Men were therefore able to give more money and gifts to their family and to other people and were consequently seen as more generous than women. They were also able to take out loans and to make savings and investments. Within the family, women were seen predominantly as mothers and usually depicted in the company of children. Men were not often portrayed as fathers and were mainly absent from the home. Instead, they belonged to the public arena, where they were largely active, energetic, rich, and successful. Women were portrayed as retiring, of minor interest, engaged in trivial activities, as serviceable (ever present in the home), dull, unintelligent, poor, largely unemployed and not mobile (they did not possess cars or use public transport).

In the science books, scientists and doctors were referred to as 'he', as were pupils. In the textbook on agriculture, despite African women's heavy involvement in food production and farming, they were rarely mentioned. In Book 3, by the end of the fourth page, a total of 129 gender specific words had been used, 128 of them male. Women were portrayed largely as carrying firewood and water.

What is important to realise when analysing texts is that the reality that they present is often a distorted one; it is the 'reality' of gendered perceptions which creates a false world in which women are largely invisible and voiceless, their share of responsibilities is downplayed, and they are reduced to a few subordinate roles. Most textbooks fail to represent the reality and diversity of both male and female roles: women are rarely presented in history, politics, or national affairs, or as heads of household, while men are rarely presented in domestic roles. Such a false portrayal deprives girls of learning from even those few positive female role models that may exist in their immediate environment, and encourages boys to believe that they must subscribe to a male myth of unflinching courage, excessive virility, and controlled emotion. Such a false portrayal prevents both boys and girls learning positive lessons from the real and evolving world around them, in which many men do spend time with their families and many women play a prominent role in public life. It also undermines the numerous efforts by agents of civil society, including women's groups, to change the very practices that the textbooks appear to be endorsing for the younger generation.

FAWE: ABC of Gender Analysis

This framework has two parts, one dealing with the text itself (presentation) and the other with the school or other educational environment in which the text is used (classroom interaction). It therefore provides the opportunity to analyse not just the written text, as Anna Obura does, but also 'the text in use', that is, the way in which the text is mediated by the teacher and learners in the context of the lesson. This latter part adds a valuable dimension – classroom dynamics – to what can otherwise be a rather mechanistic exercise of examining the inanimate written text. This framework can also be used in a selective way by teachers, trainers, curriculum developers, textbook writers, illustrators, and gender trainers.

The presentation part of the framework has two sections, narration and illustrations. This is followed by the part on classroom interaction. The first (and the most substantial) part is summarised briefly here. The full document is available on the FAWE website at www.fawe.org

Narration

To engage in a gender analysis of text, it is necessary to identify the author's position in relation to the characters and events described, and to understand the assumptions behind the voices heard. As Anna Robinson-Pant states in Sufiniso *et al.* (2000: 36) 'such in-depth deconstruction of materials is a necessary first step in working towards the production of more gender-sensitive materials, be they textbooks, newspaper reports or advertisements'. In doing this, it is important to consider what is *not* said as much as what *is* said.

The authors of the FAWE framework use the term 'narratological analysis' (drawn from Bal 1985) which recognises that any written, visualised, or broadcast (spoken) text contains within it different perspectives which mirror the reality of the subject and object: that is, that which is written about, that which is spoken about, and that which is visualised. Narration here refers to the process of presenting, representing, or making something come alive. Narratological analysis reveals how the message contained in the text is presented. In the case of a textbook, for example, learners receive the knowledge contained in the text via the author or authors. In novels, the author presents a voice that is the narrating figure.

Narratological analysis acknowledges that often there are multiple actors and voices in the same text, and that it is important to examine how the narrative has been constructed using these actors and voices. When used in the context of gender analysis, this process involves asking and responding to a series of questions that seek to reveal the gender responsiveness of the text. This does not mean that every traditional role associated with women represents a negative portrayal; so, for example, the portrayal of a woman in the kitchen is not necessarily negative. However, if women are only represented in domestic roles and not in the diversity of roles that they actually carry out in the real world, this would be considered as negative stereotyping.

The *ABC* analysis of narration is given five headings:
Action: Activities and actors are identified and quantified by gender. It is suggested that activities be categorised as productive, reproductive, or community activities.[15] Questions of workload distribution by gender should be considered, as well as the status given to individuals on the basis of the activities they perform.

Questions might include: Who acts? What kind of activities are they involved in? Who initiates what sort of action? Is there a hierarchy of activities? If so, who is at the top of the hierarchy, and why? What technology do they use and what is its nature? Does it require special skills? Who has these skills, and why?

The relationship between the helper and the helped can also be explored as an indicator of unequal gender relations. Often the person helped is in a dependent relationship to the helper; alternatively the helper may end up doing most of the work but not be recognised in this role. Questions might include: How is help defined? Who asks for and who offers help? What forms of help are there?

Locus: The location from which the actors operate is important in determining the gender responsiveness of a text. The distinction between public locus (for example, the office, the market place, the school) and the private locus (the home, the compound, the farm) is important, with the public often carrying high status whereas the private (e.g. the kitchen) is looked down upon as a 'woman's domain'. Questions could include: What is the locus of activities? What significance do places carry and why?

Visualisation: This analyses the patterns of seeing or recognising, and being seen and being recognised. It is important to identify whose view is being reported and how different players view the same matter or event. The event, situation, or object is often described by one who sees, and whose view will dominate over that of others who may also have seen but whose voice is not heard. Seeing combined with action and speech is a source of power, which can be gendered. Questions might include: Who sees and is seen? When do they see and/or when are they seen? How does this influence the direction of events?

Power: Questions of power are crucial because this defines gender relations; in particular who has power over decision making. Questions include: Who has power or is empowered? What is the source of this power? Who has power exercised over them? What is the nature of this power? How is power exercised and maintained?

Language use: Language is a powerful way of representing gender relations. In a very subtle manner, it cements the gender biases that are projected in other ways through everyday life. By engaging in this process, we can 'demystify the apparent neutrality of language through analysis of its smaller components, quantifying their appearance in texts and taking these components through rigorous qualitative analysis' (Kabira and Masinjila, 1997: 17).

The framework divides language-use into the following sections:

Naming: Naming or not naming helps shape the reader's attitude towards characters in a text. Naming a male but not a female (e.g. 'Mr Roffo and his wife') influences the reader's perception of the status accorded to each.

Questions include: Which characters are named and which unnamed? Why are some named and others not? What advantage does a name bestow on a character? How does naming or not naming contribute to the reader's general impression of the persons in the text?

Use of nouns and pronouns: how nouns and pronouns are used as a means of identifying characters. It may be appropriate to list nouns and pronouns that refer to women and men, and the order in which they appear, for example, 'he' before 'she'. Questions include: Which characters are designated by gender and which are not? Are the common nouns used in the text to refer to male and female characters? Are common nouns and pronouns (e.g. 'mankind', 'he') used to refer to both females and males? Often, male-specific nouns and pronouns are used as generic terms (mankind, chairman, businessman), which misleads the reader into thinking that women never take on these roles. At the same time, terms such as 'waitress', 'hostess', and 'actress' suggest that the female version of the male term (waiter, host, actor) is an irregularity.

Generics: words that are intended to convey gender-neutral meaning. However, they are often male terms and only include women by association and so they carry an unacknowledged gender bias. As explained above, words such as businessman, mankind, manpower, etc. are designated as male but are often intended to include women. Sometimes a gender-neutral noun is followed by a gender-specific pronoun, e.g. 'the scientist and his experiment', 'the farmer and his family'. In English it is now common practice to avoid using gendered singular pronouns by using the plural (e.g. 'they' rather than 'he/she') or the passive ('the work is done by' instead of 'he/she does the work'). It is possible to avoid the use of male nouns as generics by using a neutral noun, for example, chair person, salesperson, business people. Questions to ask include: What kind of generics are used? Are there incidents where generics are gendered? What gender-specific images does the use of generics present?

Vocatives: forms of address that bestow status on individuals, but they can also demean and patronise, for example, 'my dear lady', 'the ladies' (usually used by males towards females). Questions include: What vocatives are used and do they tell us anything about the user and the person being addressed? What impression does this create? What does their use tell us about the author's attitude towards women and men?

Other gendered references and associations: These may include derogatory connotations (e.g. women portrayed as foolish) or stereotypes (e.g. men as brave or intelligent). The personification of inanimate objects also contributes to gender stereotyping, for example, referring to a car or a ship as 'she'. Proverbs are often highly gendered; some examples are given in chapter 2.

Illustrations

The *ABC* framework has a section on illustrations, which is not covered in detail here. Pictures of all kinds present a powerful image to the reader and pass on important messages about gender relations. They often tell a story on their own, but it is also important to look at the interplay between the text and the illustrations. The illustration may be gender-neutral or gender-sensitive, but the text may lead into a stereotypical portrayal of female or male roles. For example, a father may be shown holding a baby in his arms (gender-sensitive) but the text may give the impression that holding a baby (for the camera) is enough to constitute good 'parenting'. At the same time, it is important not to read too much into pictures and not to be mechanistic in the analysis of illustrations.

Classroom interaction

The second part of the framework deals with its use by teachers and learners in the classroom context. The teacher and the learner are important mediators in interpreting the text. The categories used for this analysis are: participation of student, teachers' expectations, seating arrangements, dressing of boys and girls, teachers' behaviour, and use of space and resources. This is followed by a section entitled 'analysis and strategies'. The Commonwealth Secretariat book, in its section 'Suggestions for teachers and teacher educators', also takes classroom practice as the starting point for an analysis of the text.

Classroom setting and dynamics are crucial for teachers to address, in order to create an enabling learning environment for both girls and boys. Teachers are as central as the textbook in actively transmitting messages about gender. They can help to perpetuate biases and stereotypes or they can help to reduce them. Sunderland *et al.* (2000) provide a model of teachers 'talking around the text' in an English as a Foreign Language classroom context. In this model the teacher can either ignore traditional or non-traditional gender representation in the text, or can subvert it, or endorse or exaggerate it.

To avoid bias, teachers need to be conscious of the influence of the lesson: how it is conducted; who they turn to in the classroom; who they ask to respond to questions, what types of questions, and how often; how they respond to correct and incorrect answers; and how they convey expectations, reward, praise, reprimands, punishments, etc. For example, praise for a girl may emphasise her hard work and diligence, for a boy his creativity and initiative. Punishments may be given out differently for misdemeanours, for example, to a girl but not to a boy for swearing, to a boy for forgetting his homework. This will depend on the teacher's expectations of how each sex should behave, and what s/he considers a serious lapse in behaviour. Also, tasks set by teachers tend to be gendered: in many countries girls are required to do many chores around the school like sweeping the classroom or the yard, while boys may only perform tasks as punishments. Even the way in which boys and girls wear their uniforms and teachers' comments on whether this is appropriate or inappropriate are gender-loaded. The way female and male teachers themselves dress sends out messages about gender.

The physical space given to boys and girls (or taken by them) has an impact on the quality of learning, as does their access to resources such as books and equipment. Seating arrangements can convey gender messages, with in many cases girls sitting at the front where they are very attentive to the lesson (obedient) whereas boys sit at the back where they can chat and be disruptive ('boys will be boys') (Dunne, Leach et al. 2003). Questions that can be asked include: What resources are available to boys/girls? How are they utilised by each? What defines and demarcates the space of each and how free do they feel in their space? Does the teacher attempt to manage the way in which space is shared and controlled?

There is a great deal of research on gender in the classroom but most of it is from Europe and the USA, e.g. Arnot (2002) and Weiner (1994) in the UK. Focusing on Africa, there is the study by Dunne, Leach et al. (2003) of gendered experiences in schools in Botswana and Ghana, Anderson-Levitt and Brenner (1998) on classrooms in Guinea and Liberia respectively, Gordon (1995) in Zimbabwe, Sey (1997) in Malawi, and Maimbolwa-Sinyangwe and Chilanga (1995) in Zambia. Wamahiu (1996) writes from a general African perspective about the different pedagogies used with girls and boys in the classroom.

In summary, the *ABC* framework is a much looser framework than the previous ones, but it encourages deeper examination of the issues around the portrayal of individuals and groups in both the text and in classroom practice. There are similarities with Naila Kabeer's Social Relations Approach (rules, activities, resources, people, and power), as presented in chapter 7. Appendix 1 of the ADEA manual on gender-sensitive editing (Sifuniso et al. 2000) contains a useful checklist for assessing gender bias in written material, which combines some of the key analytical concepts of Obura's study with those of the *ABC*.

Case study 1: a primary textbook from Malawi[16]

This is an example of the analysis of illustrations, applying to a 1996 Malawi Primary textbook called *Activities with English* (Book 2) the framework from the Ukrainian UNESCO study as presented by Anna Obura. This example only covers the quantitative analysis. The analysis is incomplete without a fuller qualitative examination of the text, along the lines recommended by Obura above.

Frequency of images

There are 19 pages with pictures depicting men or boys on their own, eight depicting women or girls on their own, and 30 with both females and males depicted. In some of these, females are in the foreground, in others males are. The first named man appears on page one, the first named woman on page 19.

The ordering of images: We find on the front cover a village scene, with in the foreground a man milking a cow and a boy bringing eggs to sell at a stall by the roadside. Further back, a woman is feeding the chickens, and in the background a boy and a girl are picking fruit from a tree. The two males in the foreground are larger than the female figures behind them and are clearly the most important. While the woman is feeding the chickens (a nurturing and caring role), the boy is taking the eggs to sell (an economic activity). The second boy in the background has taken the initiative in using a stick to knock the fruit off the tree. The inside back cover shows a male tailor, that is, in an economic activity.

The first page of the book shows a picture of a male teacher standing in an authoritative position facing a mixed class of learners. The next set of illustrations to depict humans (pages 10–11) contains five drawings of people going about their jobs – all are men (shopkeeper, driver, soldier, gardener, and doctor). The first images of females are on the following pages (12–13): they show a female bus 'conductress', a female teacher, and a female typist alongside a male farmer and a male nurse, then on page 14 a male messenger, a policewoman, and a policeman.

Frequency with which individuals were named: Male characters were named 31 times and female characters 18 times (another story featured Mr Lion and other animals). In the only example of a resourceful woman (a woman who kills a snake), she is not given a name. In terms of males and females featuring in large pictures, there were eight males featured, six females and five mixed (males and females).

Positioning of images on the page: One example is given below. The lower picture depicts boys playing football and the upper one girls playing netball. The lower picture dominates the page, as it is much larger and in the foreground, while the picture depicting girls is smaller and in the background. This can send the message that the boys' game is more important or has higher status than the girls'. It also conveys gender bias in that it suggests that certain sports are only suitable for boys or girls. The location of the picture on the page also means that the boys' activity is more likely to be the focus of attention in the lesson.

Temwa and Mavuto play at school.
They play football and netball with their friends.
Temwa likes netball.
Mavuto likes football.

Work/employment images

Men are shown in eight occupations (teacher, carpenter, pilot, census officer, bus driver, police officer, storyteller, father) and women in six (fruit farmer, shopkeeper, trader, dressmaker, bus 'conductress', and mother).

Socio-political images

Men are shown as:

- having more buying power than females: a man is featured buying his daughter a dress – a generous father – opposite a girl buying two small items (salt and sugar);
- being skilled and educated: one picture depicts a census officer with a briefcase approaching two huts with three boys playing football in the foreground. No women or girls are in sight despite the caption stating that ten men, ten women, and thirty children live in the village. Another picture shows a bus 'conductress' standing outside a bus taking fares while the male driver sits at the wheel. The caption reads 'Mrs Chembe is a bus conductress. She is not a driver. She sells tickets ... ';
- in positions of authority: a grandfather is sitting on a large stone or tree trunk telling a story to a boy and his grandmother, who are both sitting at his feet in a subordinate position.

Family roles

Men appear five times as fathers, women nine times as mothers. This is an improvement on many textbooks, where men almost never appear in a family context, and women almost always do.

Psychological traits

Males are portrayed as resourceful, for example, a boy offering to mend a man's bicycle, and to carry a basket of bananas for a man. Only a picture showing a boy running away from a snake and his mother killing it suggest role reversal (brave mother, cowardly boy). Significantly, however, she is not named.

The Malawi primary textbook from which the above examples were taken was one of a series revised in 1993 with donor funding. Reducing gender bias was one of its aims, and it is true that the series represents a significant improvement on the earlier texts. For example, there are praiseworthy attempts to show women in occupational and active roles. However, their positioning and frequency in the book still suggests that they are considered less important than men and that there is still work to be done to make the texts truly gender-sensitive.

Case study 2: a primary reader for India

This is an analysis of a Grade 5 Reader belonging to an English course entitled *Gul Mohar* used in Indian primary schools and published by Orient Longman (revised edition 1997). The ABC 'narration' category of analysis is used here according to the five categories of action, locus, visualisation, power, and language use.

A quick glance at the table of contents informs us that six stories feature men or boys and only two feature women or girls, both of them about the character Pandora. According to the story, Pandora was unable to resist opening a mysterious box despite the warnings of Epimetheus, and like Eve in the biblical story she is blamed for all the misfortunes of humankind. It is only the very last story in the book, 'The Sea Monster', which has as its central character a young girl who is resourceful and ambitious. The Reader also features a number of poems, one of which is about Matilda 'who told lies and was burned to death'.

Action

There is only one story featuring an active and heroic female figure – and interestingly this is the last story in the book. Susan is a would-be journalist who engages in an adventure involving a sea monster. It is significant that she has attributes usually associated with males: bravery, physical agility (she climbs into a building from the fire escape a floor below), ambition, and initiative (she wants to be a journalist and will use desperate means to become one). She also enjoys a challenge (she goes in search of a supposed monster) and is clever (she pretends to faint to put off-guard the smuggler who is pointing a gun at her). In the other stories where women are featured in a central role, e.g. Pandora and the poem about Matilda, they are presented as foolish and/or wicked. In others, they play only a passive or peripheral role.

The stories featuring boys or men as central characters present them mostly as brave and resourceful (a story about a boy called Emil who catches a well-known thief; two young men who have a lot of adventures), as poor but resourceful (the clever shepherd who seizes the opportunity to save an abbot's life in order to improve his own position), as inventors (a doctor who invents the bicycle tyre, a doctor who invents chloroform), as hero (William Tell) or occasionally as ruthless (King John of England). In most of the stories about males, women are totally absent. Where they are mentioned, they are present in a helping and dependent capacity, and are not usually a central part of the action.

For example, in the story of Emil, his mother and grandmother are mentioned as hard working but poor, but they do not appear in the story. In another, an air hostess serves the passengers and shows kindness to the central male character by accommodating his pet (an otter). In another story about a kind and generous bishop who offers a bed for the night to an ex-convict (male), the woman is the servant who obeys orders despite disapproving of the bishop's decision. Even when the ex-convict disappears with the silver, she does not say 'I told you so', or 'I thought this would happen'. She is completely silent, a marginal figure. In a story about the American author Nathaniel Hawthorne, his wife is portrayed as resourceful, but only in so far as she had the foresight to save some of her housekeeping money over the years, so that when her husband is dismissed from his job, he can devote himself to writing. She is selfless and loyal; she saves money so that he can fulfil his yearning to be a writer. She is resourceful for his sake, not her own; she appears to have no aspirations beyond helping him.

Those who engage in activities which require skills are all male: the inventor of the bicycle tyre and the doctor who invents chloroform, and William Tell, whose prowess with the bow and arrow makes him a hero. Susan has intuition rather than skill acquired through high levels of education and training.

Locus

This Reader illustrates the importance of location in an illuminating way, in this case associated with geography not gender. All the stories are from European and North American sources and none from Asian sources, despite the fact that this is a textbook for India, a country with a rich historical tradition to draw on. This illustrates graphically the way in which certain voices dominate the text and certain types of knowledge are valued more than others. The authors of this book appear to value outside knowledge associated with rich and powerful countries more highly than indigenous knowledge. While it may be the case that the authors considered stories from the English-speaking world to be appropriate for the teaching of English, the choice sends an unfortunate message to the pupils that somehow their own heritage is not relevant in the context of teaching a world language.

In gender terms, the locus of the stories reveals women to feature largely in the private domain of the home, with exceptions being Susan the journalist and the air hostess. Men are featured in both private and public locations.

Visualisation

In terms of whose views are being reported, the story about a man called Maxwell who takes his pet otter in a box onto a plane exemplifies how influential this is. The man finds himself sitting next to a 'very well dressed and dainty looking American lady', who remains totally silent throughout the story. Although the air hostess speaks to her, her words are not reported. Even though the pet otter empties her travelling bag while she is asleep, she is given no opportunity to react to this. The final paragraph reads 'But what did the lady say or do when she opened the bag and discovered the mischief? Maxwell never got a chance to find this out. In a short time the aircraft landed in Cairo and the lady left.'

No women are portrayed in public roles apart from Britain's Queen Victoria (who appears briefly in the story about the doctor who invented chloroform) and the would-be journalist Susan.

Power

Power is clearly invested in the male characters; only Queen Victoria is a powerful female character but we do not see her exercising it beyond allowing the new drug chloroform to be given to her before an operation and later conferring the title 'Sir' on the doctor who administered it. Despite being a queen, she is true to the female stereotype in expressing gratitude to the male character for 'the great relief that his drug had brought her'.

Language use

Because of the structure of the Reader, where a narrative (story or poem) is presented and comprehension and grammar exercises follow, these exercises inevitably also feature male characters as they are based on the preceding narrative. In this way, male pronouns, and adjectives and adverbs describing male characteristics, predominate. Even where the exercise is not linked to the story, male examples abound, on page 22, for example, the nouns and adjectives for ruler, wealth, power, loyalty, popularity, and pride are all associated with male characters, including famous public figures (Gandhi and Nehru – the first Indian figures to be mentioned). Occasionally, there is a widening of female roles in the exercises, e.g. a female doctor.

So, to young learners this Reader presents a world peopled predominantly by men, who are resourceful, brave, wise, and generous; occasionally ruthless and stupid. Women are either totally absent, or are on the margins of this world as supporting and servicing men in a domestic setting. In two out of the three narratives featuring females, they are portrayed as stupid and troublesome. On the whole women voice no opinions, they are silent and obedient; men issue instructions and women obey; men act and decide; women know their place. The would-be journalist is presented as an exception, operating according to male rules in a male-dominated world.

Proposals for improvement (drawn from Brickhill, Obura, and the ADEA manuals)

Obura provides a list of techniques for improving the accuracy of textbook images of girls and women. These are classified as avoiding bias (avoidance techniques); and encouraging positive images of all people (positive techniques). The UNESCO gender-sensitivity manual also provides examples of positive and stereotyped portrayal with suggestions of good practice. Brickhill et al. (1996) suggest the following as strategies to reduce gender bias: role reversal, role balancing (between males and females), assertiveness of female role models (giving them greater prominence), and deliberately changing the stereotypical associations with certain roles (e.g. by locating women more often outside the home than inside).

The ADEA manual provides many useful strategies for professional textbook writers, editors, and designers to reduce gender stereotyping; in particular the chapter on 'Gender bias in illustrations' which contains sections on 'types and purposes of illustrations', 'selecting illustrations', and 'gender issues in artwork'. Likewise, the chapter on 'Principles of design' contains sections on design and typography (typeface). It is important that curriculum panels and watchdog committees also receive training in what they should be looking for when told to eliminate gender bias: it is ignorance of the scale and scope of the stereotyping rather than resistance to being gender-sensitive that perpetuates the negative images.

The recommendations are condensed as follows:

Avoidance techniques: avoiding gender-biased language

- Avoid gendered singular pronouns: e.g. the English *he* and *she;* use the gender-neutral plural *they* instead.
- Avoid gendered singular nouns where they are not necessary: *boy, girl, woman, man, etc.* Use gender-neutral nouns in the plural if necessary: *children, people, parents;* or gender-neutral singular nouns: *head teacher* or *the head* not *headmaster/headmistress, chairperson* not *chairman/woman, parent* not *mother* or *father, child* not *girl* or *boy.*
- Use collective nouns (*the class, the group*).
- Use impersonal verbs (e.g. 'it is easy to make'), imperatives ('take the books') or passive verbs (e.g. 'the cows are milked')

Positive techniques: encouraging positive images

- Deliberately portray women and girls in a wide range of positive roles.
- Apply role-reversal to portray males and females in atypical roles (e.g. a boy cooking, a woman driving the car).
- Balance male and female roles carrying out tasks together (e.g. both male and female teachers, taxi drivers, nurses).
- Increase reference to women and girls; increase first appearance, order of presentation, and centrality of female characters. Make female characters the centre of a story.
- Increase the number of named female characters and the use of female descriptions.
- Make a balanced presentation of relationships between characters regarding dependency, authority, etc.
- Portray women with positive character traits: resourceful, responsible, creative, intelligent, etc.

- Increase the portrayal of women in the public sphere – in economic and political roles as well as social, and in leadership roles (member of parliament, director of a company, head teacher etc.).
- Increase female role models, with particular reference to female participation and achievement in science, technology, agriculture, computer science, the professions, and leadership roles.
- Place greater emphasis on female intellectual and professional capacities.
- Increase portrayal of males in the private domain, in a family capacity, and sharing domestic duties.

Anna Obura recommends the inclusion of a greater number of female- than male-related images so as to counteract the centuries of bias in educational textbooks and materials. Greater use can be made of feminine words where this can have a positive impact, for example, 'business woman', 'a scientist/lawyer/farmer ... she ... '. She is of the opinion that, even though it goes against the principle of using gender-neutral nouns where possible, this strategy will make readers conscious that when reading words like 'farmers', 'scientists', 'doctors', 'officials', they are *both* female and male.

Illustrations

The UNESCO manual provides examples of ways in which we can ensure a balanced portrayal in the use of illustrations (UNESCO 1997: Section 8).

- Have illustrations which include both male and female: boys and girls playing together rather than separately, with girls being as adventurous as boys (e.g. climbing a tree).
- Avoid stereotyped family scenes such as the women cooking and the man reading a newspaper, the boy playing football while the girl mends clothes or fetches water. Instead, show the man playing with the children or working in the kitchen, the woman reading the newspaper or playing with the children; show the girl playing football and the boy mending clothes; or show both parents playing, reading, sharing domestic and childcare responsibilities, both the girl and the boy mending clothes, etc.
- Avoid portraying boys as active and girls as passive, e.g. the boy rowing the boat while the girl sits and gazes around (have both rowing, or rowing in turns).
- Avoid stereotyped pictures of occupations and activities: show a female pilot or engineer, or a male nurse or nursery or primary teacher; avoid girls playing only with dolls, and boys with play bricks or cars.
- Provide an equal balance of female and male characters in the foreground: the man should not always be the one facing the picture in a central position at the front of the picture, with the woman to the side or at the back; the man should not always be in a leadership role in pictures

portraying groups, e.g. walking along a road or working in a field in front of women. Placing women in a central position suggests they are also in control and strong.

Portraying girls/women as well as boys/men in strong, central, leadership roles can have a powerful effect on girls' aspirations. Portraying boys/men in family roles, sharing domestic responsibilities will also help to dispel the image that this is somehow 'unmanly' and that only women are intended for 'nurturing' and 'caring' roles.

Obura also points out that the same principles apply to other sources of bias, ethnicity, for example. All too often in textbooks certain ethnic groups are associated with certain traditional practices and occupations: pastoralists are always portrayed with cattle, *Inuit* (previously called Eskimos by outsiders) with husky dogs and sledges, coastal people with boats and fishing nets. A modern nation should allow all its peoples access to technology, adequate shelter, education and health services; they should therefore be portrayed in a range of activities. All groups need positive examples, which combine a respect for tradition with opportunities for improved lifestyles.

Commentary

Uses

These tools can be used by a wide range of people working in an educational context.

The benefits of the analysis rapidly become clear. Even analysing a small section of a text, e.g. one unit or chapter, brings out the extreme gender bias so often present, both in terms of the stereotyped characteristics associated with female and male, and the silence around women's activities and roles.

Facilitating action: The analysis can be an activity carried out by pupils themselves, as part of an awareness raising activity.

The analysis makes a direct route to action readily identifiable, usually through the revision of textbooks to eliminate bias.

Limitations

It can be time-consuming and mechanistic; there is a risk that a gender analysis is narrowed down to little more than counting numbers of female and male images and names.

It is often difficult to capture the overall impression of the book; this is not easily communicated through identifying and analysing separate elements such as numbers of images, references to females or males in the text, and use of gendered terms.

The learning context: Revision of textbooks does not ensure that they are used in a gender-sensitive way or that opportunities to discuss gender issues are engaged in by teachers and learners. Most analyses (excepting the FAWE *ABC* and the Commonwealth Secretariat manual) exclude an examination of the textbook in use, which is in fact just as important as the text itself. A gender-unaware text can be used in a gender-sensitive way if stereotypes are picked up and discussed during the lesson, and vice versa.

Further reading

Anderson-Levitt, K.M., M. Bloch and A.M. Soumare (1998) 'Inside classrooms in Guinea: girls' experiences', in M. Bloch, A. Beoku-Betts and B.R. Tabachnick (eds) *Women and Education in sub-Saharan Africa: Power, Opportunities and Constraints*, Boulder, Colo.: Lynne Rienner.

Brenner, M.B. (1998) 'Gender and classroom interactions in Liberia', in M. Bloch, A. Beoku-Betts and B.R. Tabachnick (eds) *Women and Education in Sub-Saharan Africa: Power, Opportunities and Constraints*, Boulder, Colo.: Lynne Rienner.

Brickhill, P., C. Odora Hoppers and K. Pehrsson (1996) *Textbooks as an Agent of Change: Gender Aspects of Primary School Textbooks in Mozambique, Zambia and Zimbabwe*, Education Division Documents No. 3, Stockholm: Sida.

Commonwealth Secretariat (1995) *Gender Bias in School Text Books*, London: Commonwealth Secretariat.

Dunne, M., F. Leach et al. (2003) *Gendered Experiences: the Impact on Retention and Achievement*, London: DFID.

Sifuniso, M., C. Kasonde, E.N. Kimani, I. Maimbolwa-Sinyangwe, W. Kimani and M. Nalumango (2000) *Gender-Sensitive Editing*, London: Working Group on Books and Learning Materials, Association for the Development of Education in Africa (ADEA).

Sunderland, J., M. Cowley, F. Abdul Rahim and C. Leontzakou (2000) 'From bias "in the text" to "teacher talk around the text": an exploration of teacher discourse and gendered foreign language textbook texts', *Linguistics and Education*, 11(3): 251–86.

Weiner, G. (1994) *Feminisms in Education: an Introduction*, Buckingham: Open University Press.

9 | Participatory tools for analysis and action

Introduction

There are very many examples of tools using a participatory format that are appropriate for gender awareness raising activities and for assisting in the development of strategies for change. Those associated with what is known as Participatory Rural Appraisal (PRA) use visual representation as the stimulus for participatory activities. PRA was first developed as a means of promoting community involvement in the development process, but it is also appropriate for addressing gender inequalities. The more recent adoption of the term Participatory Learning and Action (PLA) illustrates the potential of participatory tools for educational contexts. The literacy programme *Reflect* (which features in chapters 5 and 6 of this book) employs a participatory methodology coupled with Paulo Freire's theoretical framework.

Sources

This chapter is not intended as a comprehensive guide to the range of participatory tools that can be used in an educational setting, nor does it suggest that these tools can be used effectively without specific training. Rather it provides a 'taster' of the wide range of resources that are available. If you are serious about learning how to use such tools, you should look at the range of source books detailed in the bibliography and seek training from an experienced facilitator or practitioner. In particular, Robert Chambers' book *Participatory Workshops: a Sourcebook of 21 Sets of Ideas and Activities* provides a wealth of advice and plenty of examples of disasters. It is intended for broad use by teachers and trainers as well as for conference and workshop organisers and facilitators. As Robert Chambers says, it is 'for all who try to help others learn and change' (2002: xi). Chambers groups his ideas under the following headings: brief basics; beginning, middle and end; messing up; groups, seating and size; analysis and learning; and behaviour and awareness. He also lists sources of ideas for trainers and facilitators and adds a note on equipment, materials, and furniture. The PRA website (www.ids.ac.uk/ ids/particip), the *Reflect* website (www.reflect-action.org), and the website of the International Institute for Environment and Development (www.iied.org/resource) all provide useful information and free downloadable material. For participatory work around the particularly sensitive topic of sexual relationships and HIV/AIDS, the widely used *Stepping Stones* approach for working with adults (Welbourn 1995) offers a step-by-step guide which can be applied to a range of settings.

The examples provided below are drawn from a few of the many source books that exist: Rachel Slocum *et al.* (1995) *Power, Process and Participation*; ActionAid's *Reflect Mother Manual: a new approach to adult literacy* by David Archer and Sara Cottingham (1996), an ActionAid paper by Kate Metcalfe entitled '*Reflect*: towards a Gender and Development Approach', and Oxfam's *Gender Training Manual* (Williams 1995). With the exception of the last two, none of the above sources addresses gender specifically, but they are sensitive across all social categories, and so can be used with any social grouping.

As already explained in chapter 5 in the context of the *Reflect* programme, discussion and analysis of local issues is prompted by the construction of visual material such as maps, matrices, calendars, diagrams, time lines, etc. Central to PRA methodology is the belief that ordinary people are capable of critical reflection and analysis and that their knowledge 'counts' (Chambers 1997). Participatory activities give voice to those who may otherwise be excluded from decision making and the control of resources. In addition to the construction of a series of graphics which reflect their own local reality, participants can generate non-graphic work such as drama, role plays, songs, story telling, photography, and video.

Participation in this context refers to the active involvement of people in making decisions about the implementation of processes, programmes, and projects which affect them. In short, its purpose is to promote equal participation in the benefits of the development process. It is usually linked to the concept of empowerment, so that in PRA work, for example, the process of constructing visual materials is not an end in itself but a means to the end of helping people to take greater control over their lives. It is the participants' analysis of and reflection on their own social, economic, and political circumstances and the subsequent discussion of how these can be changed for the better that is crucial. Change will usually be achieved through gaining greater access to political processes and to resources, whether these are in the form of knowledge and information, or financial or material resources. Behind this is also the assumption that strengthening people's involvement in problem-definition, data-collection, decision making, and implementation will facilitate capacity building, and build confidence, consensus, and accountability within communities.

Limitations of the participatory approach

However, as has already been pointed out in chapters 1 and 6, the reality of both 'participation' and 'community' is often far removed from the ideal. Marc Fiedrich and Anne Jellema (2003:III) have pointed out that expectations about the influence of participatory activities on lasting change in people's lives are often unwarranted. Even more alarming, the scale of participation and the motive for doing so can also be questioned. In their 2002 study of *Reflect* literacy programmes, they state that:

> ... *claims of 'empowerment' made on behalf of most participatory methodologies, including Reflect, are often empirically exaggerated and internally contradictory. Although participatory approaches are often presented as a fundamental break with 'top-down', ethnocentric paradigms of development, aid agency reports tend to suggest that Reflect participants spontaneously adopt the very same attitudes and practices long championed by the development community.*

> *While* Reflect *practitioners' accounts emphasise how participants 'take control of their own lives', learners are more likely to anticipate prestige and material rewards from association with a rich and powerful institution. Few practices in the classes would have given learners reason to assume that that they were involved in anything radically different from 'school' or 'education'.*
Executive Summary

In similar vein, John Pryor (2002) in his research into understandings of education in a village in rural Ghana points to the over-romanticised view of communities as being built around consensus. Some communities can be very fragmented along ethnic, religious, and class (and in some cases race and caste) lines; others have poorly developed civil society organisations. Given that much current policy on education (especially where it is constrained by a Structural Adjustment Programme) is built around aspirations of increased community participation in all aspects of educational provision, this suggests an unrealistic aim. Indeed, there is evidence that these aspirations are often interpreted as the requirement that parents pay fees and other levies only; other aspects of community participation such as involvement in decision making and monitoring within the school through parent-teacher associations or school-management boards have been much less effective – and not always welcome by head teachers and education officials.

It is important to recognise diversity in all its forms; every community contains power imbalances and a range of personal viewpoints and convictions that make genuine consensus difficult. Trying to see a 'group' or a 'community' as a homogenous entity can be seriously misleading. Moreover, participatory methodologies may ignore social relationships within communities and so exclude particular social groups whose voice is not heard as loudly as others or not heard at all, for example, women, disabled people, the old, children. Most communities contain individuals and groups with an inadequate voice in decision making. Even though participation is likely to be uneven, most development workers subscribe to the principle of genuine participation while recognising that it is open to manipulation by development agencies and other interested parties wishing to gain credibility for their proposals and programmes. The concept itself covers a continuum of approaches and aims, ranging from small-scale efforts at increasing the share of resources among marginalised groups to radical redistribution of wealth. If we use participatory tools with an awareness of their limitations, they can be highly effective in terms of raising awareness, developing a sense of individual and social responsibility, and building the capacity for change. However, they cannot of themselves bring about desired change and we also need to recognise this when we develop aims for participatory work. This applies to their use within an educational setting as much as in other spheres of social and community life.

It should be noted that PRA methods are used to cover a wide range of issues around development. They have not been designed specifically for gender analysis and gender-awareness raising work. It is therefore important to ensure that you ask appropriate questions and design activities that will prompt an exploration of gender issues. The gender analysis frameworks outlined in the earlier chapters of this book can help you to do this.

Many of the PRA-type activities listed below can be used with adult literacy groups, and some have been designed specifically for this purpose. Groups can be single sex or mixed, divided by age, ethnicity or race, according to the nature of the activity and the extent to which the community feels comfortable within a mixed group. It is often more productive to start with single sex groups, so once the women have become more confident about voicing their opinions, they can be brought together with the men. The same applies to working with children. It may be sensible to start activities with individuals or small groups, as even within apparently homogenous groups such as illiterate women in a village, there is a power hierarchy that allows some to speak and obliges others to remain silent.

A warning

PRA is seductive in its simplicity and in the immediate results that it can produce in terms of raising awareness and a desire for change, but it can easily be used unwisely, especially where it intrudes on personal emotions. Attractive though these tools may be, it should always be remembered that they are potentially exploitative, in particular when confidentiality is promised. Facilitators can extract a great deal of information through a process which often entertains, distracts from daily burdens, and makes people feel secure in a group. What people do with the information gained is crucial; if not handled sensitively, it can ruin lives. The process can easily become manipulative, even coercive. Children are particularly vulnerable to such exploitation as they are trusting and open in what they say.

Workshops

Participatory tools can be used in many different settings but they are most commonly used in a workshop format. The decision to run a workshop will be made according to a specific set of circumstances and may be instigated by an outside agency, with invitations to an identified group of people to attend, or by a group of individuals who wish to retain ownership of the whole process themselves. In all cases, however, the designated participants need to be involved in setting the aims and outcomes of the event, and where appropriate in aspects of organisation; this includes school pupils and children. At the risk of unwarranted generalisation, a number of principles can be listed, with a view to preventing negative consequences.

- Make the whole process as inclusive as possible – practise what you preach on participation.
- Ensure that everyone is clear about the aims of the workshop, in both the short and the longer term; don't try to do too much.
- Think carefully about whom to invite and how many: do not invite too many participants unless you are very experienced; do not exclude people who should be involved because they are less visible or accessible.
- Think carefully about your own role: participatory approaches do not allow you to dominate, criticise, or direct events in a way that you might wish to in other contexts. Running a workshop on your own is difficult, so involve other facilitators.
- Decide on an appropriate venue: if you are handling a sensitive topic, always hold it away from prying eyes and ensure confidentiality at all times.
- After discussing and agreeing with others, decide on the language to be used during the workshop, and the cost, the duration, and materials. Having one or more rapporteurs to keep notes of the proceedings is very helpful.
- Make sure that the question of follow-up is addressed, and who will be involved in it.
- Consider drawing up a protocol or code of conduct for the workshop, so that all involved will know what is acceptable and what is not (for example, what you will do if the process becomes too intrusive and upsetting for one or more individuals).

If you are inexperienced at using participatory tools and are unable to obtain formal training, you can practise on a group of colleagues or friends first, or seek help from an experienced local facilitator to try out your activities first.

With these reservations in mind, a small selection of participatory tools are presented below. They have all been chosen from the wide range available for their appropriate use in educational contexts; whether for use with adult learners as part of a literacy programme, or with pupils, teachers, or parents and other community members as part of an initiative to increase awareness of some particular aspect of education. Examples include HIV/AIDS education with pupils and/or teachers, raising awareness in the community of the importance of sending children to school, or providing them with sufficient time for homework. The examples drawn from a study into the abuse of girls in African schools were all carried out with pupils. Children find the production of visuals particularly engrossing.

Some of the activities can be carried out in conjunction with the frameworks that have featured in chapters 3–6.

Participatory tools

Maps

Village or household maps, where the group draws a map of their village with all the houses marked, are often useful to examine the division of labour, access to health services, water supplies, etc. In an educational context, school maps can be used to illustrate the gendered roles of teachers and pupils (for example, who is in a powerful or leadership role, who chairs committees, who gets the tea, who runs sports events, who counsels pupils, who has budgetary control). Such a map could be integrated into an analysis using the Harvard Framework, showing the gendered structures of the organisation in visual form. The *Reflect Mother Manual* suggests that school mapping can also be used to identify existing educational resources or opportunities and to develop consensus as to what more is required. So, for example, they could start by identifying how many members of the community have passed through each level of education (primary, secondary, university, technical). This could lead to a discussion of what further educational provision is required (e.g. a secondary school, a school library, a locking storeroom in the existing school) and, in the case of a new school, its best location. This information can then be used to lobby local officials.

The *Reflect Mother Manual* suggests a further exercise involving a mapping of literacy in the community. Such a map might start with a map of the village and the identification of places where the written word is seen in public. Often participants will not 'see' all the written materials around them because they are very familiar. So a walk through the village to identify written materials such as posters, shop signs, and signposts will draw attention to the extent to which this may be a literacy rich – or poor – community. Participants can then follow this with a household map of literacy materials to identify what written materials they have in the home, e.g. on medicine bottles, fertiliser packs, food products. Once this is complete, a discussion can be held on the importance of creating a more literate environment in order for children and adult learners to consolidate what they learn. This might be done by setting up rural libraries, community noticeboards, wall newspapers, etc.

Calendars

A gender workload calendar is useful for analysing the sexual division of labour. The work carried out by women and by men is documented separately across the months, allowing for an examination of the various roles and responsibilities carried out by each sex. It offers the opportunity to consider whether the current division of labour is fair, and helps to raise awareness about the multiple roles of women and the heavy and often unrecognised workload associated with their reproductive role. It may result in some sharing of domestic duties with men such as fetching water or firewood, or looking after children. A study of the impact of participatory activities on a number of rural settled communities in Kenya and Tanzania (including a refugee camp) found that there was increased understanding and critical awareness of the burden of women's heavy workloads, with some men starting to share responsibilities traditionally considered to be exclusively female such as cooking, feeding children, and taking children to the health clinic (Masoy and Pridmore 1997).

A calendar can also be a record of daily activities. This can be applied to a school setting, for example, to examine the impact of multiple roles on female and male teachers' school work. A school-term calendar can be used to map female and male responsibilities for times when there are meetings, parents' days, exam setting, prize giving, etc. An annual calendar can be used to log the impact of child labour on school attendance over a whole year, highlighting seasonal changes in workload patterns (see the example in Table 9.1). This might lead to a decision to lobby for a shorter school day during busy seasons such as harvest time. Completing the calendar could involve questions such as

- What tasks are girls/boys involved in outside school? Why?
- Which is the busiest time of year for girls/boys? Why?
- What status is attached to each type of work? Why?
- What do they learn from the work they do?
- What is the effect of this work on girls'/boys' learning?
- How much time does each have for homework?

Table 9.1 Childrens gender workload calendar

	Girls				Boys				
	Domestic	Fetching firewood	Fetching water	Selling vegetables	Bird scaring	Weeding	Harvesting	Paid labour	Herding
Jan									
Feb									
Mar									
Apr									
May									
Jun									
Jul									
Aug									
Sep									
Oct									
Nov									
Dec									

It can also be useful in helping to determine appropriate school terms and vacations, and also the most suitable hours for schooling or literacy programmes, where such issues can be decided flexibly. Many NGO- and community-run school programmes adopt flexible school hours, for example, BRAC in Bangladesh which features in chapter 4 provides schooling for only three hours a day and at times mutually agreed between the teacher and the parents. Information from such a calendar could influence district, regional, or national education officers to consider changes to the fixed timetable in an effort to get more children into school.

A calendar could also be incorporated into an analysis using the Harvard Framework or the GAM (where gendered activities and roles and responsibilities are identified).

Trees

Trees can be used to identify patterns of income and expenditure, with the roots as income and the branches as expenditure (they are also used to identify sources and uses of credit). This can be applied to education, for example, to assess how much is spent on girls and boys in a household and the impact that this has on school attendance. A girl's uniform is often more expensive than a boy's and so the girl may be withdrawn from school if the family cannot afford the uniform.

The problem tree is another common PRA tool, with the roots as causes of the problem, and the branches as the consequences. This can be applied to any aspect of education, such as the under-representation of girls in school or high truancy among boys. In many ways it is similar to a SWOT analysis (see below), and can even serve as a much simpler version of the tool used in the Social Relations Approach (chapter 7) to unpack the causes and effects of a structural problem. An example of a problem tree is provided later in this chapter.

SWOT

SWOT (Strengths, Weaknesses, Opportunities, and Threats) analysis is used extensively in many contexts. It is not necessarily used in a participatory mode, but it does lend itself particularly well to workshop formats. It is an appropriate tool for a whole range of educational situations, and in general terms it is useful when thinking about the difficulties of change, identifying possible strategies to bring about change, and helping to formulate action plans. The process of bringing about change in gender relations in an organisational setting might involve, for example, creating a new policy, project, or programme which seeks to incorporate gender targets. It is intended to help people identify *internal* strengths and weaknesses and *external* opportunities and threats through a series of guiding questions directed at identifying key issues.

Table 9.2 A SWOT analysis chart

Strengths	Weaknesses
Opportunities	Threats

This analysis can lead to the development of an overall strategy or set of strategies and an action plan. An example is provided in chapter 4.

A variation of this is to present a chart mapping the driving and the restraining forces that influence the extent to which a particular goal may be reached (called a 'force field analysis'). If the restraining forces outweigh the driving forces, the desired change will be doomed, unless the stakeholders can work to reduce the negative forces and boost the positive forces, by mobilising political support or lobbying local authorities, for example.

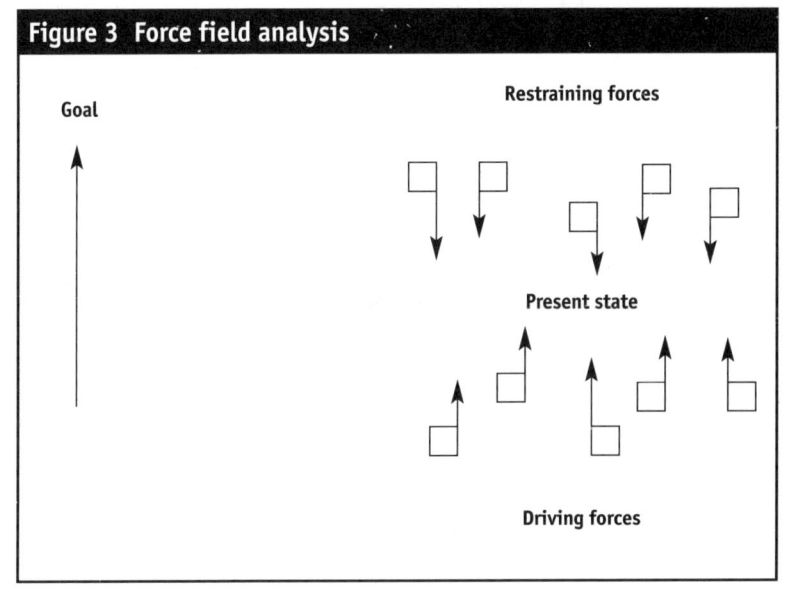

Figure 3 Force field analysis

Goal

Restraining forces

Present state

Driving forces

Adapted from Whitaker, 1993

Venn diagrams

These are usually applied to illustrate the relationships between organisations (they are also called *chapati* in Asia and *tortilla* in Latin America). In a community context, participants can draw a map of their village or community and identify all the organisations that exist within it, such as school, village committee, church, mosque or temple, sports clubs, women's groups, and cooperatives (see Figure 4). Each organisation can be represented by a circle, with the size of the circle reflecting the importance attached to the organisation, and the participants determining the criteria by which they judge this. When used for the purpose of gender analysis, the numbers of women and men involved in each organisation, and their roles and responsibilities can be discussed, as can their perceptions of the organisations and those who speak at meetings, decide the agenda, and take decisions. This can lead to a discussion of who is excluded from these organisations, whose discourse dominates them, and the timing and conduct of meetings. A Venn diagram can also indicate which of the organisations they think are the most important, which have the respect and confidence of the villagers, and who participates and is represented in each. It can also help to identify organisations outside the community that can be lobbied or involved in bringing about change. Links can be indicated between community organisations, and between community and other external organisations working together. (This can be done by using lines or arrows of different width or size to represent degree of importance, or through two or more circles overlapping). If the detail provided in the Venn diagram is sex-disaggregated or is provided separately by men and women, it will show not only how membership of organisations is biased but also how access to them and the power that they wield is determined. For example, a group of women may have no connection at all with outside organisations, while men do, and in this way they are able to influence priorities for funding and other resources.

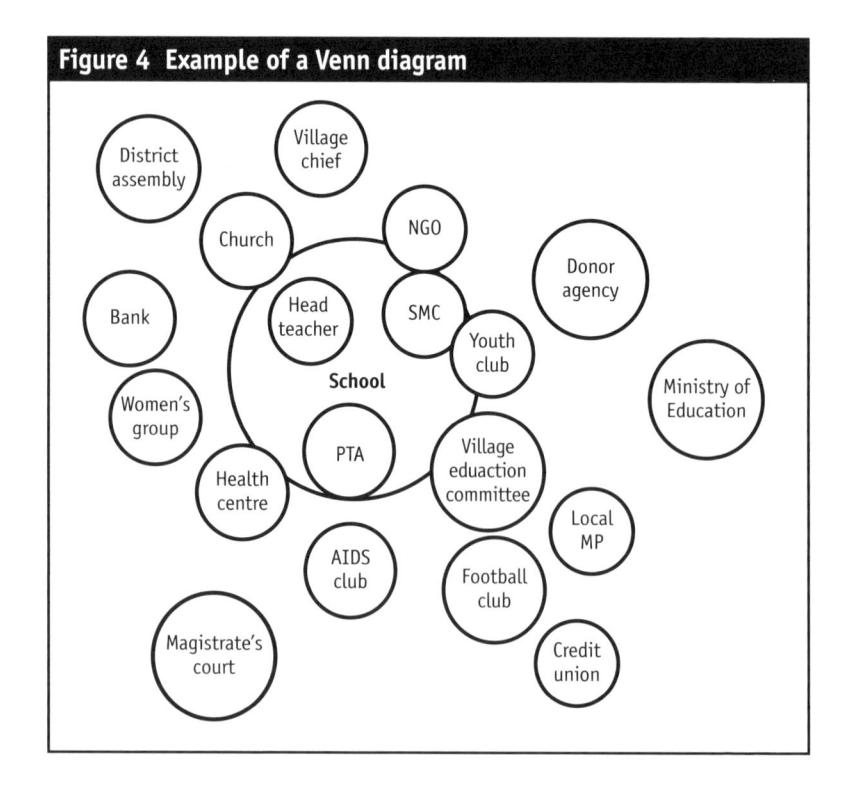

Figure 4 Example of a Venn diagram

This activity could also be carried out as part of a literacy class, teaching new words while also increasing awareness of how power is distributed within the community according to gender, ethnicity, class, wealth, etc. Another example might be where the community identifies all those individuals and organisations that influence school provision, and signals by the size of the Venn circle their relative power over the school. So, for example, the following might all be represented by circles of varying size: the PTA, school-management board, local chief(s), district officials, inspectors, government political representatives, local politicians, magistrates, wealthy landlords, chiefs and elders, health officials, donor agencies, and NGOs. When seeking to bring more resources into a school, the Venn diagram will help them identify where they need to lobby for support or to apply pressure. This may be different for different purposes, for example, if they wish to secure electricity for the school, this will require lobbying different individuals or organisations than if they require more textbooks, or if they wish to have a head teacher removed. This can be an exploration of gendered power, as it is likely that most or all of those who are identified as influential are male. It can also be done in a more sophisticated way to look at how gender intersects with other social indicators to provide advantage and privilege. Applied internally within a school setting, it can be used to examine the way in which gender roles and responsibilities are allocated and the power associated with them, as a means of awareness raising and promoting equal opportunity.

Pie chart

A pie chart could be used to examine how funds are spent, for example, at the school or the district-office level. The pie represents the total available, and 'slices' may be marked as salaries, books, furniture, sports day, etc. This would also show how power is distributed according to who has access to these funds and also whether female pupils and staff and male pupils and staff benefit equally from the expenditure.

Activity profile

This is an alternative to the Venn diagram and is adapted from a gender analysis activity profile in Slocum *et al.* (1995: 100–02). It is a simpler version of the Harvard framework presented in chapter 4. It is used to raise awareness about who is responsible for which activities in a community, and why. The participants are asked to list all community activities, identifying who is responsible for each and then examining why particular individuals or social groups (characterised by gender, race, class, age, etc.) do particular tasks. The division into reproductive, productive, and community roles is useful here (an example is shown in Table 9.3).

Table 9.3 Gender activity profile: community involvement in education

Activity	Who decides?	Who does it?	Why?	What is the impact?
Building classrooms				
Helping with repairs				
Fundraising				
Committee member				
Paying school fees				
Helping in classroom				
Helping with sports				
Helping with school and community events				

This activity can be applied to community involvement in education, for example the group lists all the activities engaged in by the community with regard to schooling. This might include:

- construction (of buildings, classrooms, toilets);
- school maintenance;
- fundraising;
- village education or school committee;
- parent–teacher association;
- giving talks, presentations, or demonstrations;
- helping with teaching or extra-curricula activities.

They can then examine who is involved in each of these, why and how they got involved (whether they were elected, volunteered, persuaded by village elders, etc.), who makes decisions relating to the activities, and the extent to which these are embedded in gender roles. The impact that their involvement or non-involvement has on their children's education can also be examined. This activity could be usefully applied to the case study from Tanzania (chapter 5), where it appears that women most frequently make the school contributions for their children, but have little or no voice on school committees.

Role play

Role play can offer invaluable opportunities for raising sensitive issues around gender and identifying key problems in a non-threatening way. As Robert Chambers (2002: 138) says: 'Role plays and theatre open up wonderful scope across the whole range of learning, analysis and exploring realities and implications. In role play and theatre there is special licence: the unsayable can be said; the hidden can be revealed; power can be mocked and made to laugh at itself. By acting out situations, people can uncover and discover aspects otherwise overlooked or unknown'. It is particularly effective when seeking to address sensitive issues and behaviour change, for example in sexual behaviour, perhaps in relation to HIV/AIDS.

Pupils and adults can act out role plays about their lives – these may reveal domestic violence, sexual abuse, alcoholism, bullying at school, excessive workloads, differentiated opportunities and expectations, and the impact of poverty on females and males. Females may act out male roles or vice versa. As Kate Metcalfe suggests in her paper on gender and *Reflect*, participants can act out a recent scene from a soap opera, which can lead to an analysis of the roles and relationships usually carried out by females and males; it may also lead to an interesting examination of gender roles in relation to other social indicators such as class or wealth. Folktales and traditional stories such as myths, legends, and fairy stories offer endless opportunities for an analysis of gender roles and relationships. For example, the evil characters are often female (witches, stepmothers, 'ugly' sisters, and other sadistic old women), and the heroine of the story (usually young and beautiful) is always rescued by a man (usually young and handsome), without whom she would be locked in misery, captivity, or an enchanted sleep for eternity.

Role plays, as with all participatory activities, can be misleading, however. As already pointed out, participants may experience rapidly raised levels of self-confidence and strong convictions about how to change their lives, which may not be lasting. The 'buzz' usually disappears quite rapidly as the difficulties of implementing the good intentions become real. The case study in Box 3 provides one example of how follow-up and evaluation can make a short-term activity to raise awareness and change behaviour have a more lasting impact.

> **Box 3 Mobilising Young Men to Care**
>
> Dramaide, a South African NGO, and the University of Natal worked with groups of students in two Durban schools to develop plays designed to raise awareness about HIV/AIDS and gender. Afterwards, the team engaged the students in a piece of evaluative research in which they reflected on the process of developing the role plays. In doing this, it deepened the impact of the role plays on their attitudes and behaviour. The team worked with both boys and girls, but the focus was on changing male behaviour.
>
> The evaluation team worked with both single-sex and mixed groups, discussing the impact of the drama work by focusing on the changes in their understanding about gender equality. These 'conversations' allowed the learners to reflect critically on their lives with a new-found awareness of their gendered selves. By building up a strong rapport with the learners in this way, the team was able to challenge entrenched ideas about gender inequality. Girls in particular were able to 'test' their new understandings, for example the realization that it was not obligatory to have sex with an assertive boy or to do the bidding of a fellow male learner, and in this way to challenge pervasive gender relations. For boys, the work led them to take more responsibility for their actions, to be more able to express emotions and to develop an understanding, at least, of the possibility of 'doing masculinity' differently. The process enabled the learners to evaluate themselves through a process of self-reconstruction. The girls in particular were much clearer about themselves, their rights, their position as women, the impact of gender inequalities historically upon their lives, and committed to asserting themselves more forcefully in social and educational contexts in the future.
>
> Interviews following this activity revealed that despite the focus on male learners, the biggest impact was among female learners. They became more expressive, outspoken, and confident in challenging exploitative and uneven gender parameters within intimate relationships. They insisted on being consulted and respected by boys and by friends and teachers. Boys became more reflective and open to ideas of gender equality in their own lives and relationships.

Source: Morrell (2002), accessed from www.id21.org/education/gender_violence/index.html

Time line

A time line is used to record important historical markers in a community or organisation. This can provide a useful starting point for discussing changes in gender perceptions, roles, and relationships over time, as well as future developments. In an educational setting, it can be applied to female and male involvement in a school over time, perhaps in raising money for construction or for a teacher's salary, or in monitoring school attendance through regular home visits. Such an activity can raise awareness about the relative contributions and improved understandings of the roles that women and men play in the school and suggest ways in which these roles could be made more gender-equitable or enhanced in some respect. A gender-sensitive time line can map how gender roles have changed over the period, and the causes and outcomes of this. It can also be used to identify ways in which the management of the school has changed, perhaps as a result of the establishment of a parent–teacher association; or how a new curriculum has changed the school culture, perhaps by the introduction of life skills as a subject with its implications for teaching about sexual and gender relations; or how the school as an organisation has changed over the years, marking major events and changes in direction. This process would help identify strengths and weaknesses of what has been achieved to date and indicate areas for improvement over the coming years. These changes in gender relations might be mapped in terms of access and control of school resources, decision making, tasks, and responsibilities.

Matrix

A detailed matrix has been presented in chapter 6 (Rani Parker's Gender Analysis Matrix). This is designed for complex monitoring over time and along a number of dimensions. A simpler version of a matrix is suggested in Table 9.4 as a literacy or awareness raising activity (adapted from one in the *Reflect Mother Manual*: 187–91). In this example, it identifies who goes to school at each level or grade, and examines why some children drop out or never enrol.

The instructions from the *Reflect Mother Manual* are to construct a matrix with the appropriate school levels on the horizontal line and age groups on the vertical line, with these divided into male and female. The horizontal line might be as follows:

X (means that this person has never been to school) / lower primary / upper primary / lower secondary / upper secondary / college / university.

The exact levels chosen will depend on the educational system. For a more detailed survey, for example, if schooling stops at the end of primary or junior secondary, it may be appropriate to identify each grade rather than each level.

Ask each participant to consider their own household as you go through the age groups. If they have a girl or a boy in that age range, they should put a mark in the appropriate place to show the level or grade they are now in. If there is a non-formal centre as well as a formal school, this should be covered separately – two coloured pens could be used to make the marks. Where a child has never been to school, that also needs to be recorded.

Once the matrix is completed, the marks in each box can be added up and the numbers written down. The completed matrix will then be used to invite discussion around why some children are not in school, why some often play truant and why some have dropped out. This analysis might then lead to a campaign to raise funds for the school, to improve attendance, or to set up a PTA or school or village education committee.

Table 9.4 Education matrix

Age group	No education	Lower primary grades 1–3	Upper primary grades 4–6	Lower secondary grades 7–9	Upper secondary grades 10–12	College/ University
5–8 M	•••••••••••	•••••••••••••••••••••				
F	•••••••••••••	•••••••••••••				
9–12 M	•••••	•••••	•••••••••••••••••••••••••••••	•••		
F	•••••••••••••	•••••••••••	••••••••••••••••••			
13–15 M	•••••••••••••		•••	•••••••••••••••••••		
F	•••••••••••••••••••		••	•••••••••••••••		
16–18 M	•••••••••••••••••			•••••••	•••••••••••••••••••	••••••••
F	•••••••••••••••••••••••			•••••••••••••••••	••••	•••
19–29 M	••••••••••••••••••••••					••••••••
F	•••••••••••••••••••••••••••••••••••					••••

Other suggestions for using matrices are made by Archer and Cottingham in the *Reflect Mother Manual* (pp. 230–32), for example, to identify local people who can act as a resource to the school, as helper, additional teacher, running workshops, giving talks, or carrying out repairs, to support curriculum development and to map literacy in the home and community.

Action plans

Action plans can take many forms and like SWOT analyses do not necessarily have to be developed in participatory mode. Some are based around specified aims and objectives, detailing the action to be taken and by whom, desired outcomes, and the person(s) responsible for monitoring them. A simple format suitable for an organisational action plan is shown in Table 9.5. This can be modified to serve as a personal action plan.

Table 9.5 Organisation action plan

	Within the next few days	By ...	By ...
We will:			
We will need to talk to:			
We need to get help and/or support from:			

A more detailed version is shown in Table 9.6.

Table 9.6 Organisation action plan

Identified need/ objective	Desired outcome	Agreed actions	Who organises	Resources required	Timescale	Who monitors

Participatory tools for analysis and action | 141

Case study: pupils' workshop materials on abuse in African schools

The following examples are drawn from a research study funded by DFID during 1998–2000 into the abuse of girls in African schools.[17] This study investigated abusive behaviour and sexual violence towards girls in a number of junior secondary schools in three countries (Ghana, Malawi, and Zimbabwe). The main perpetrators were male pupils, male teachers, and older men in the vicinity of the school who proposition young schoolgirls for sex (often called 'sugar daddies'). PRA workshops were held either at the start or at the end of the research, in order to explore problems that both boys and girls experienced at school, and in particular to uncover the pattern and extent of abusive behaviour perpetrated against girls.

Each workshop was held over two days in the schools where the researchers had conducted the fieldwork and had interviewed pupils, teachers, and parents. The pupils were aged 13–15. The first day of the workshop was spent exclusively with girls; the first part of the second day was spent with boys on their own, who were then joined by the girls. The girls ended the workshop on their own with some role plays. Around 15 girls and 10 boys participated in each workshop. Each day started with 'energisers' and warm-up activities in the form of songs and games, and regular short breaks were held for relaxation and further songs. Pupils were given snacks and drinks. Coloured pens, large sheets of paper, and colourful cards and stickers were used throughout. Some examples of the pupils' drawings are shown below.

A brief account follows of the PRA activities used in the workshops and how they were used. The account follows the order in which the activities were carried out at the time.

School maps

In small single-sex groups of four to five, pupils were asked to draw a map of the school and the surrounding area and use stickers of different colours to indicate areas where they felt safe and areas where they felt unsafe (green for 'safe', red for 'unsafe'). They could use all their stickers and distribute them as they wished. The groups then came together to discuss the maps, giving reasons for their choices. By asking girls and boys to draw maps separately, it was possible to compare sources of anxiety. Both girls and boys felt unsafe in certain locations, for example, outside the school boundaries, near the staff room and school office, but girls on the whole identified a greater number of areas where they felt unsafe: this included the toilets, the school garden, and the playing fields, where they were accosted by boys. In particular, it emerged that boys waited to catch girls on their way to and from the toilets, and attempted to touch their breasts, spy on them, and even assault or rape them.

Figure 5: Example of a school map

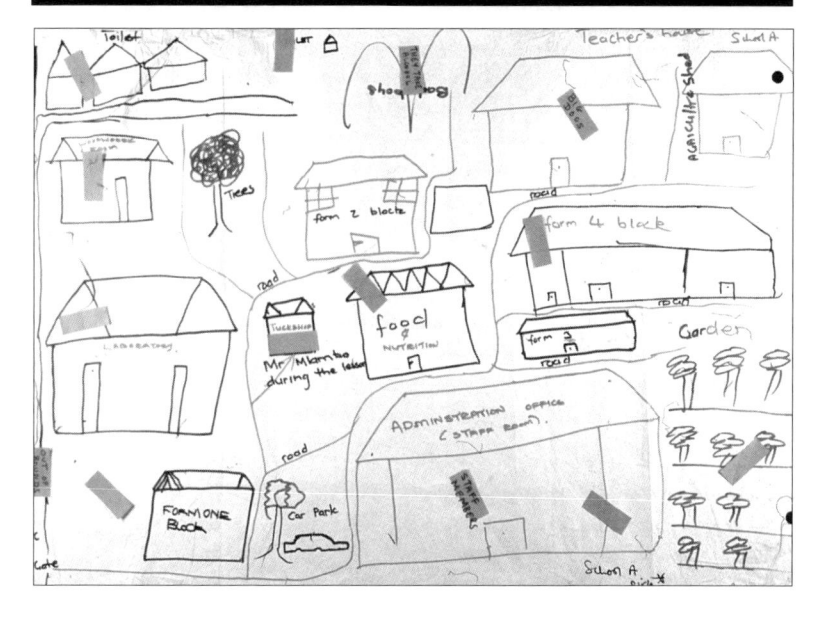

'Abuse' spiders

The scale of abuse in the schools emerged when the pupils in single-sex groups were asked to draw a spider with each leg indicating the type of abuse that existed in and around the school (see Figure 6). Each pupil in the group was given a set of 20 sticky dots and asked to place them where s/he thought the abuse was most serious. Both girls and boys identified being beaten excessively by teachers as a serious and frequent form of abuse. Girls also identified being touched on their breasts or buttocks by boys and male teachers, while boys cited being forced to smoke marijuana and drink beer by older boys around the school premises. Boys also admitted that girls were subject to much sexual harassment, and sometimes rape.

Problem trees

The pupils were then asked to draw a 'cause and consequence' tree with roots as causes and branches as consequences. Two single-sex groups were asked to address the double question 'Why do boys have sex with girls? Why do girls have sex with boys?' and another two groups were asked 'Why do teachers have sex with girls? Why do girls have sex with teachers?'.

When asked to indicate why a girl would have sex with a teacher, both girls and boys indicated that girls wanted money to buy things like chocolate and

Figure 6: Example of an 'abuse' spider

sweets at break time, or to pay school fees. They might also want to show off or do what they think other girls are doing. Because of the fear of AIDS, teachers would want to have sex with young girls whom they thought were free of the disease. Teachers might also want sex with young girls because they envied their youth and carefree lives. As consequences, the girl might get pregnant, but the teacher would not leave his wife for her if he were married; the girl might also get a sexually transmitted disease or AIDS. The girl would be expelled and she might end up committing suicide, or dumping the baby. The teacher might also be dismissed.

When asked why boys wanted sex with girls, alongside the suggestion that boys wanted to experiment, to make girls lose their virginity, and to have proof that the girl loved him, both girls and boys expressed the notion that boys wanted to 'fix' the girl, that is, place her under his control, to show that he was a man and in some sense to 'punish her for being female'. As for a girl, she might have sex with a boy because she needed money, but also because she might want him to marry her or to show her genuine feelings.

Figure 7: Example of a problem tree

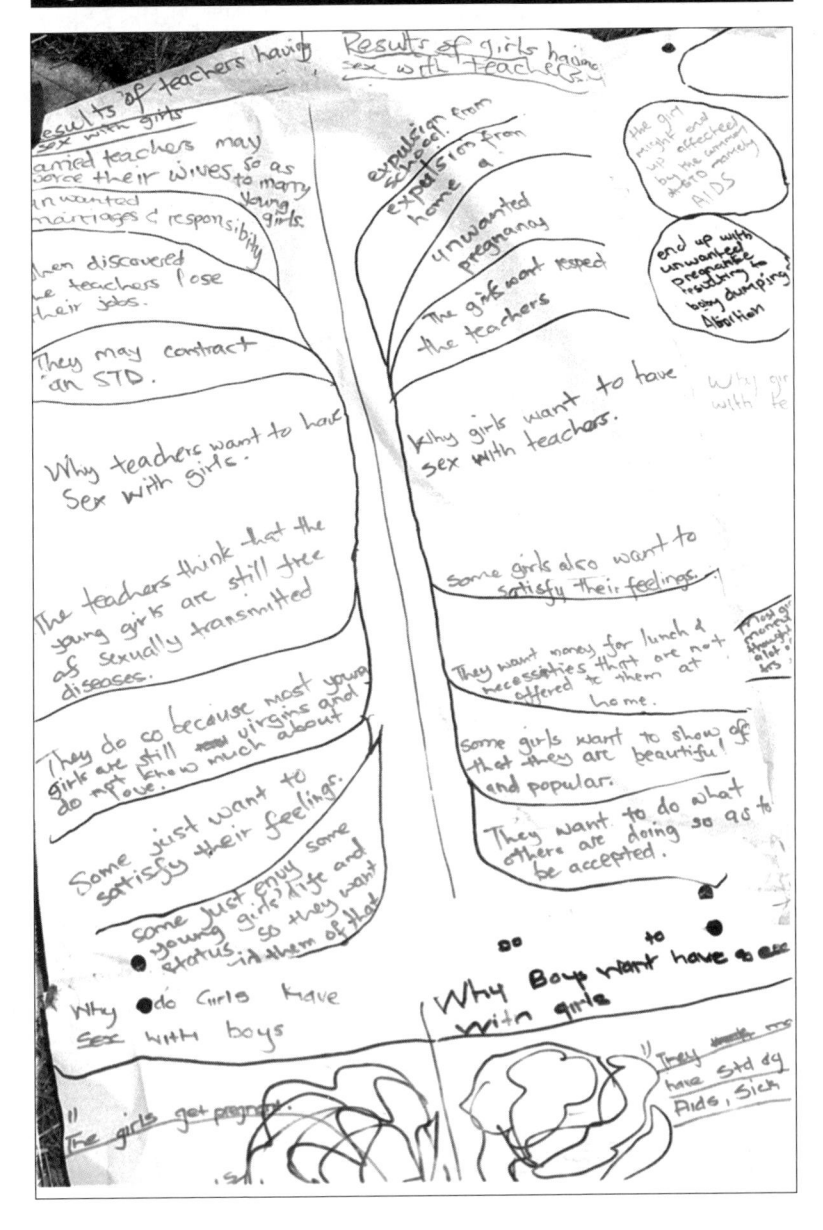

Role play

Girls prepared some very realistic role plays about the abuse they experienced in and around the school. One portrayed a male teacher who used his position to abuse girls in his class; if the girl fell for his sexual favours she would be given pocket money and be the teacher's favourite, but if she declined he would use any pretext to beat her. Another group showed how a teacher's attention was focused on one particular girl in the class: the teacher passed comments on how smart the girl was, patted her, and tried to straighten her blouse so as to touch her breasts. The class showed that they knew what was going on by booing and hissing loudly when he asked her to come to the front of the class to read, and when he praised her after she had read a passage badly. He detained her after class, sent her to buy something for him, and asked her to bring books to his office so that he could engage her in conversation and try to touch her. He gave her money, which she boasted about to a friend. Despite being advised against going with a teacher, she ignored her friend; but when she told the teacher she was not interested any more, he told her that she could not refuse because he had given her money. She either had to pay him the money back or have sex with him.

Another play vividly depicted the harassment that girls in a peri-urban school went through on a daily basis as a gang of boys lay in wait for them in the bushes leading away from the school. The boys pounced on the girls, whistling at them, grabbing their breasts, and locked them in an embrace which they struggled against. Other boys stood around and laughed.

Problem walls

Pupils wrote on a card a problem they experienced, repeating the process for every problem they could think of. Only one problem was allowed per card. The cards were stuck on the wall of the classroom. They were then grouped under different headings like 'beatings by teachers', 'touching by teachers', 'boys proposing', etc., and then prioritised. One group of girls' prioritisation is as follows (in decreasing order of importance, with some items given equal ranking):

1 dumping babies (i.e. getting pregnant and abandoning the baby)
2 forced to be in love with teachers/forced to be in love with Form 4 boys
3 touching by boys/touching by teachers
4 abusive language by teachers/beatings by teachers
5 pupils smoking and drinking
6 shortage of textbooks and chairs/teachers coming late to lessons

Those problems mentioned the most on the cards were not necessarily ranked the highest.

The researchers and the girls then discussed the problems and ranked them according to which were easy to solve and which were difficult. They looked at how they could best be solved, classifying them as strategies to be undertaken 'by us', 'with us', and 'for us'.

Solution circles

This is a more detailed form of strategy identification to follow on from the problem wall. In some workshops, the girls drew concentric circles and labelled them as they discussed strategies to solve the problems detailed on the problem wall. They discussed where the solution to each problem lay, in terms of 'me' and 'other pupils' at the centre, then the school (committee and teachers), the family, and the community in expanding outer circles. They then placed a card in the relevant circle. If the solution lay at two levels, they placed the card between the two. Their suggestions for what they themselves could do included: supporting each other; refusing to see a male teacher on his own; moving around the school with other girls to reduce the opportunity of assault by boys; and reporting cases of abusive behaviour to the head teacher or to their parents. As for what the school could do for them, they wanted boys who assaulted them to be punished, teachers who were known to make proposals to girls to be dismissed, and corporal punishment reduced.

It was striking how in all the schools the girls saw themselves as primarily responsible for their own problems, whether it was school failure, pregnancy, or being beaten. Thinking of appropriate action to take either alone or with the assistance of someone else was therefore the most difficult part of the workshop for them. On the whole, the girls gave the impression that they thought such problems were an inevitable part of school life that had to be suffered. They had not considered that they had any rights, or that anybody should be expected to do something about their situation. Their knowledge of where responsibility should lie was therefore very limited, that is, whether it should be their parents, or the school, the community, or the government who should take action, and what action was appropriate. However, in the follow-up period of research, when the girls were given opportunities to engage in further participatory activities including writing stories and poems, analysing scenarios and case studies, and taking part in local and national discussions on the topic of abuse, they gained a 'voice' with which to articulate their own understandings of their situation. They showed themselves in this way to be capable of analysing their situation skilfully and making sensible and creative suggestions about the ways in which the school environment could be improved for their benefit.

Commentary

Uses

Most of these participatory activities require limited resources and can be done anywhere, outdoors or indoors.

They can be used with both adults and children, in single-sex or mixed groups. They engage both children's and adults' interest easily; they are fun.

Using such tools, key issues and problems emerge very rapidly and can be addressed directly. They are particularly effective for raising awareness (although topics like domestic abuse, rape, AIDS, etc. are very sensitive and need to be carefully addressed).

Participatory work provides space for critical discovery, self-analysis, and reflection. When used effectively, it can be genuinely uplifting as it gives voice and space to people not usually accustomed to them.

Limitations

PRA-type work needs a trained and experienced facilitator; if misused, it can be intrusive, exploitative, and manipulative.

If sensitive topics are not handled well, individuals may become distressed or disturbed by the process, as it touches a raw nerve or awakens unwelcome memories.

It tends to ignore the fact that some voices are louder than others and therefore count more; failure to analyse power relations can entrench powerful players further.

PRA activities are usually public events – many people, especially women, lack the confidence to speak in public and are placed at a disadvantage.

It may encourage the notion that a false consensus exists or that consensus is essential, when it is often unobtainable.

If PRA work is used in the context of a research study, it should be used alongside other data-collection techniques, e.g. interviews or questionnaires. It cannot on its own accurately assess the scale of an issue.

Follow-up: PRA work should not be used unless there is a strong commitment by all those involved to act upon the conclusions reached, and by those initiating the activities to continue to support the group in reaching the goals they have helped them to identify.

After the excitement of a PRA workshop or other participatory event, action may be much more difficult back in the real world. It can generate a temporary and false self-confidence, and so it is dangerous to rely on such work on its own to bring about change. Monitoring and follow-up are crucial.

The focus on what is in the public domain ignores the private domain. This is especially important for women, and key structural problems around household relations may not be included in any needs assessment or plan of action.

Further reading

Chambers, R. (1997) *Whose Reality Counts? Putting the First Last,* London: Intermediate Technology Publications.

Masoy, A. and P. Pridmore (1997) 'Participatory learning and action to reduce women's workloads in East Africa', *International Journal of Educational Development,* 17/1: 51–7.

Notes

1 The more common term 'gender blind' is avoided here as it suggests that people without sight are in some way less aware of gender issues than others, which is clearly not the case.
2 Jayaweera's (1997) study of the relationship between education and the UNDP's indicators of women's economic, social, and political empowerment in 24 Asian countries found no positive linear relationship.
3 Medical advances which have made routine sex change operations possible, and even the not so distant likelihood of cloned humans, somewhat blurs the clarity of this male-female distinction, as does sexual orientation (bisexuality, transgender, etc). However, the fact remains that only a woman who is born a woman can give birth.
4 This is a term used by Naila Kabeer (see note 13).
5 *The Oxfam Gender Training Manual* (1995) and March *et al.* (1999) have slightly modified versions.
6 Sources for this case study are BRAC NFPE Annual Report 1997, BRAC Programme Proposal NFPE Phase 2, 1998/9, and BRAC Education Programme Annual Report 2002 supplemented by personal communication.
7 The project has since been re-oriented to focus on the professional development of teachers.
8 ActionAid(1999) 'Evaluation of *Reflect* programme in Bunkpurugu, East Namprusi', p. 10.
9 Sources for this case study are: Leach, F. *et al.* (2000b) *The Impact of Training on Women's Micro-enterprise Development,* and Leach, F. and S. Sitaram (2002) 'Micro-finance and women's empowerment: a lesson from India'.
10 ActionAid: *Reflect* Pilot Project End Evaluation, Part 1, June 2001.
11 Stromquist uses the term 'institution' here to refer to schools, in contrast to Kabeer who would use the term 'organisation'.
12 This case study draws on material provided by Hyde *et al.* (2001) *The Impact of HIV/AIDS on Formal Schooling in Uganda,* which is part of a Rockefeller-funded research study into HIV/AIDS and schooling in three Sub-Saharan African countries. It also draws on two articles: Mirembe and Davies (2001)

'Is schooling a risk? Gender, power relations and school culture in Uganda', and Mirembe (2002) 'AIDS and democratic education in Uganda'.

13 Naila Kabeer also draws a distinction between policies that are gender-blind (gender-unaware) and those that are gender-aware; she subdivides the latter into three types: gender-neutral, gender-specific, and gender-redistributive (these differ from those more widely used, which are contained in the list of definitions in chapter 2). Gender-redistributive interventions are intended to transform existing distributions of resources to create a more balanced relationship between women and men, either by targeting women or men or both. Affirmative action to get more women into certain jobs, or into management positions would be gender-redistributive. In an educational context, some governments have introduced quotas of places reserved for female students or for female teachers, or have set lower grades for girls' progress to the next stage of education, usually from secondary into higher education.

14 The texts are listed in Obura (1991: x–xii).

15 These are Caroline Moser's three categories of gender roles (see chapter 2).

16 *Activities with English for Malawi: Pupil's Book 2*, revised edition 1996, Blantyre: Macmillan.

17 Sources for this case study are: F. Leach, *et al.* (2000c) 'A Preliminary Investigation of the Abuse of Girls in Zimbabwean Junior Secondary Schools', and F. Leach, *et al.* (2003) *An Investigative Study of the Abuse of Girls in African Schools*.

Bibliography

ActionAid (2001) 'Malawi *Reflect* Pilot Project: End Evaluation: June, Report (Part 1)', ActionAid Malawi.

ActionAid (1999) 'Evaluation of *Reflect* Programme in Bunkpurugu, East Namprusi, March 8–10, Bimomba Literacy and Farmers Cooperative Union (BILFACU)', ActionAid Ghana.

Anderson-Levitt, K.M., M. Bloch, and A.M. Soumare (1998) 'Inside classrooms in Guinea: girls' experiences', in M. Bloch and F. Vavrus (eds.) *Women and Education in Sub-Saharan Africa: Power, Opportunities and Constraints*, Boulder, Colorado: Lynne Rienner, pp. 99–130.

Archer, D. and S. Cottingham (1996) *Reflect Mother Manual: a New Approach to Adult Literacy*, London: ActionAid.

Arnot, M., J. Gray, M. James, and J. Ruddock with G. Duveen (1998) *A Review of Recent Research on Gender and Educational Performance*, OFSTED Review of Research, London: The Stationery Office.

Arnot, M. (2002) *Reproducing Gender: Essays on Educational Theory and Feminist Politics*, London and New York: RoutledgeFalmer.

Bal, M. (1985) *Narratology: Theory of Narrative*, Toronto: University of Toronto Press.

Bernstein, B. (1996) *Pedagogy, Symbolic Control and Identity: Theory, Research and Critique*, London: Taylor and Francis.

Bourdieu, P. and J.C. Passeron (1977) *Reproduction in Education, Society and Culture*, London: Sage.

BRAC (2002) 'Education Programme Annual Report 2002', accessed from www.brac.net

BRAC (1998) 'Programme Proposal NFPE Phase 2, 1998/9', Dhaka: BRAC.

BRAC (1997) 'Annual Report NFPE', Dhaka: BRAC.

Brenner, M.B. (1998) 'Gender and classroom interactions in Liberia', in M. Bloch, J.A. Beoku-Betts, and B.R. Tabachnick (eds.) *Women and Education in Sub-Saharan Africa: Power, Opportunities and Constraints*, Boulder Colo.: Lynne Rienner, pp. 131–56.

Brickhill, P., C. Odora Hoppers, and K. Pehrsson (1996) *Textbooks as an Agent of Change: Gender Aspects of Primary School Textbooks in Mozambique, Zambia and Zimbabwe*, Education Division Documents No. 3, Stockholm: Sida.

Castells, M. (1997) *The Power of Identity*, Oxford: Blackwell.

Chambers, R. (1997) *Whose Reality Counts? Putting the First Last*, London: Intermediate Technology Publications.

Chant, S. and M. Gutmann (2000) *Mainstreaming Men into Gender and Development: Debates, Reflections, and Experiences*, Oxfam Working Papers, Oxford: Oxfam.

CIRAC (2001) 'Global Survey of Reflect, Paper 2', CIRAC (International Reflect Circle), (accessed from www.reflect-action.org).

Commonwealth Secretariat (1995) *Gender Bias in School Textbooks*, London: Commonwealth Secretariat.

Cornwall, A. (2000) 'Missing men? Reflections on men, masculinities and gender in GAD', *IDS Bulletin*, 31(2): 18–27.

Cornwall, A. (1998) 'Gender, participation and the politics of difference', in I.Gujit and M. K. Shah (eds.) *The Myth of Community: Gender Issues in Participatory Development*, London: Intermediate Technology Publications, pp. 46–57.

Derbyshire, H. (2002) *Gender Manual: A Practical Guide for Development Policy Makers and Practitioners*, DFID Issues series, London: DFID.

Dunne, M., F. Leach with B. Chilesa, T. Maundeni, R. Tabulawa, N. Kutor, D. Forde, and A. Assamoah (2003) 'Gendered experiences: the impact on retention and achievement', London: DFID.

Fiedrich, M. and A. Jellema (2003) *Literacy, Gender and Social Agency: Adventures in Empowerment*, London: DFID.

Forum for African Women's Educationists (FAWE) (1997) *The ABC of Gender Analysis*, Nairobi: Regal Press.

Foucault, M. (1974) *The Archaeology of Knowledge*, London: Tavistock.

Freire, P. (1970) *Pedagogy of the Oppressed*, New York, NY: Continuum.

Global Coalition for Education (2003) 'A Fair Chance: Attaining Gender Equality in Basic Education by 2005', Global Campaign for Education (accessed from www.campaignforeducation.org).

Gordon, R. (1995) *Causes of Girls' Underachievement: the influence of teachers' attitudes and expectations on the academic performance of secondary school girls*, Harare: University of Zimbabwe.

Hyde, K., A. Ekatan, P. Kiage, and C. Barasa (2001) *The Impact of HIV/AIDS on Formal Schooling in Uganda*, Brighton: Centre for International Education, University of Sussex.

Jayaweera, S. (1997) 'Women, education and empowerment in Asia', *Gender and Education*, 9(4): 411–23.

Joshi, G.P. and J. Anderson (1994) 'Female motivation in the patriarchal school: an analysis of primary textbooks and school organisation in Nepal, and some strategies for change', *Gender and Education*, 6(2): 169–82.

Kabeer, N. (1994) *Reversed Realities: Gender Hierarchies in Development Thought*, London: Verso.

Kabeer, N. and R. Subrahmanian (1996) 'Institutions, Relations and Outcomes: Framework and Tools for Gender-Aware Planning', IDS Discussion Paper 357, Brighton: Institute of Development Studies.

Kabira, W.M and M. Masinjila (1997) *ABC of Gender Analysis*, Forum for African Women Educationalists (FAWE), Nairobi, Regal Press.

King, E.M. and M.A. Hill (1993) *Women's Education in Developing Countries: Barriers, Benefits and Policies*, Washington D.C.: World Bank.

Leach, F. (2000a) 'Gender implications of development policies on education and training', *International Journal of Educational Development*, 20(3): 333–47.

Leach, F., S. Abdulla, H. Appleton, J. el-Bushra, N. Cardenas, K. Kebede, V. Lewis, and S. Sitaram (2000b) *The Impact of Training on Women's Microenterprise Development*, DFID Education Research Report No. 40, London: DFID.

Leach, F., P. Machakanja with J. Mandoga (2000c) *A Preliminary Investigation of the Abuse of Girls in Zimbabwean Junior Secondary Schools*, DFID Education Research Report No. 39, London: DFID.

Leach, F. and S. Sitaram (2002) 'Micro-finance and women's empowerment: a lesson from India', *Development in Practice*, 12(5): 575–88.

Leach, F., V. Fiscian, E. Kadzamira, E. Lemani, and P. Machakanja (2003) *An Investigative Study of the Abuse of Girls in African Schools*, London: DFID.

Longwe, S. (1991) 'Gender awareness: the missing element in the Third World development project', in T. Wallace and C. March *Changing Perceptions: Writings on Gender and Development*, Oxford: Oxfam.

Longwe, S. (1998) 'Education for women's empowerment or schooling for women's subordination?', *Gender and Development*, 6(2): 19–26.

Mac an Ghaill, M. (ed.) (1996) *Understanding Masculinities*, Milton Keynes: Open University Press.

Maimbolwa-Sinyangwe, I.M. and B.Y. Chilangwa (1995) 'Learning from Inside the Classroom: a research report', Lusaka: UNICEF and Ministry of Education, Zambia.

March, C., I. Smyth, and M. Mukhopadhyay (1999) *A Guide to Gender-Analysis Frameworks*, Oxford: Oxfam.

Masoy, A. and P. Pridmore (1997) 'Participatory learning and action to reduce women's workloads in East Africa', *International Journal of Educational Development*, 17(1): 51–7.

Metcalfe, K. (2001) '*Reflect*: towards a Gender and Development Approach', unpublished paper for ActionAid.

Mirembe, R. (2002) 'AIDS and democratic education in Uganda', *Comparative Education*, 38(3): 291–302.

Mirembe, R. and L. Davies (2001) 'Is schooling a risk? Gender, power relations and school culture in Uganda', *Gender and Education*, 13(4): 401–16.

- Molyneux, M. (1985) 'Mobilization without emancipation? women's interests, state and revolution', *Feminist Studies* 11(2).

Morrell, R. (2002) 'Mobilising Young Men to Care', accessed from www.id21.org/education/gender_violence/index.html (June 2003).

- Moser, C. (1993) *Gender Planning and Development: Theory, Practice and Training*, London: Routledge.

Nath, S.R. (2002) 'The transition from non-formal to formal education: the case of BRAC, Bangladesh', *International Review of Education*, 48(6): 517–24.

Newbigging, A. (2002a) 'How can Education Advisors help to achieve the PSA Gender Equality Targets? Guidance sheets for promoting equal benefits for females and males in the Education Sector', DFID Education Department, London: DFID.

Newbigging, A. (2002b) 'A Mapping of Gender Training and Awareness-raising Activity for Education Professionals across 14 Donor Agencies in the UNGEI Network', London: DFID.

Obura, A. (1991) *Changing Images: Portrayal of Girls and Women in Kenyan Textbooks*, Nairobi: African Centre for Technology Studies.

Overholt, C.A., M.B. Anderson, K. Cloud, and J.E. Austin (1985) *Gender Roles in Development Projects: a Case Book*, West Hartford CT: Kumarian Press.

Oxfam (1999) 'Tanzania Primary Education Project', Oxford: Oxfam.

Parker, A.R. (1993) *Another Point of View: a Manual on Gender Analysis Training for Grassroots Workers*, New York, NY: UNIFEM (also available from Women Ink, New York).

Pryor, J. and J.G. Ampiah (2002) 'Understandings of Education in an African Village: the Impact of Information and Communication Technologies', DFID Education Report, London: DFID.

Rahman, Z.H. (1998) 'Non-formal primary education: a gender-based programme', in P. Drake and P. Owen *Gender and Management Issues in Education: An International Perspective*, Trentham Books.

Rose, P. (1995) 'Female education and adjustment programs: a crosscountry statistical analysis', *World Development*, 23(11): 1931–49.

Rowlands, J. (1999) 'Empowerment examined', in D. Eade (ed.) *Development with Women*, Oxford: Oxfam. (This paper was first published in *Development in Practice* 5(2), in 1995.)

Sey, H. (1997) 'Peeking through the Windows: Classroom Observations and Participatory Learning for Action Activities (COPLAA)', Arlington VA: Institute for International Research.

Sifuniso, M., C. Kasonde, E.N. Kimani, I. Maimbolwa-Sinyangwe, W. Kimani, and M. Nalumango,. (2000) *Gender-Sensitive Editing*, Working Group on Books and Learning Materials, Association for the Development of Education in Africa (ADEA).

Stromquist, N.P. (1997) 'Gender sensitive educational strategies and their implementation', *International Journal of Educational Development*, 17(2): 205–14.

Stromquist, N.P. (ed.) (1998) *Women in the Third World: an Encyclopedia of Contemporary Issues*, New York, NY: Garland.

Sunderland, J., M. Cowley, F. Abdul Rahim, and C. Leontzakou, (2000) 'From bias "in the text" to "teacher talk around the text": an exploration of teacher discourse and gendered foreign language textbook texts', *Linguistics and Education*, 11(3): 251–86.

Terry, G. (2001) 'How to Challenge a Colossus: engaging with the World Bank and the IMF', Gender and Development Network, WOMANKIND Worldwide.

UNDP (2002) *Human Development Report*, New York, NY: UNDP.

UNESCO (1997) *Gender Sensitivity: a training manual*, Literacy Section, Basic Education Division, Paris: UNESCO.

UNESCO (2002) *Education for All: Is the World on Track*, EFA Global Monitoring Report, Paris: UNESCO.

Wamahiu, S.P. (1996) 'The pedagogy of difference: an African perspective', in P.F. Murphy and C.V. Gipps (eds.) *Equity in the Classroom: towards Effective Pedagogy for Girls and Boys*, London: Falmer Press/UNESCO, pp. 46–58.

Walkerdine, V. (1988) *The Mastery of Reason*, London: Routledge.

Wallace, T. and C. March (1991) *Changing Perceptions: Writings on Gender and Development*, Oxford: Oxfam.

WCEFA (1990) 'World Conference on Education for All: Final Report', Jomtien: Inter-Agency Commission.

Weiner, G. (1994) *Feminisms in Education: an Introduction*, Buckingham: Open University Press.

Whitaker, P. (1993) *Managing Change in Schools*, Buckingham: Open University Press.

Williams, S. with J. Seed and A. Mwau (1995) *The Oxfam Gender Training Manual*, Oxford: Oxfam.

Willis, P. (1977) *Learning to Labour: How Working Class Kids get Working Class Jobs*, Farnborough: Saxon House.

Young, M.F.D (ed.) (1971) *Knowledge and Control: New Directions for the Sociology of Education*, London: Collier Macmillan.

Sources on participatory methods

ACORD Eritrea (1995) *Training Manual in Community Development: a Practical Guide for Trainers of Trainers and Practitioners in Community Development*, London: ACORD.

Archer, D. and S. Cottingham (1996) *Reflect Mother Manual: a New Approach to Adult Literacy*, London: ActionAid.

Chambers, R. (2002) *Participatory Workshops: a Sourcebook of 21 Sets of Ideas and Activities*, London: Earthscan.

IIED *PLA Notes (participatory learning and action)*, regular free publication available from IIED, www.iied.org.bookshop/ email: subscription@iied.org

Kaner, S., with L. Lind, C. Toldi, S. Fisk, and D. Berger (1996) *Facilitator's Guide* to *Participatory Decision Making*, Gabriola Island, BC, Canada: New Society Publishers.

Pretty, J.N., I.Gujit, I. Scoones, and J. Thompson (1995) *Participatory Learning and Action: A Trainer's Guide*, London: International Institute for Environment and Development.

Slocum, R., L. Wichhart, D. Rocheleau, and B. Thomas-Slayter (eds.) (1995) *Power, Process and Participation – Tools for Change*, London: Intermediate Technology Publications.

Welbourn, A. (1995) *Stepping Stones: a package for facilitators to help you run workshops within communities on HIV/AIDS, communication and relationship skills*, London: ActionAid (available from TALC, PO Box 49, St Albans, Herts, UK).

Wilcox, D. (1994) *The Guide to Effective Participation*, London: Partnership Books.

Websites on participatory methods

www.ids.ac.uk/ids/particip
Includes links to other participation websites.

www.reflect-action.org

Websites on gender and education

www.campaignforeducation.org
The website of the Global Campaign for Education.

www.girlseducation.org
Resources for policy makers and practitioners to promote girls' education, set up by an inter-agency group comprising DFID, World Bank, UNICEF, and Rockefeller Foundation.

www.genie.ids.ac.uk
A gender-equality mainstreaming website funded by DFID in partnership with the Institute for Development Studies, Sussex; includes an education section.

www.ids.ac.uk/bridge
A website specialising in gender and development; includes education sources.

www.undg.org
The UN Girls' Education Initiative website.

www.worldbank.org/gender/relatedlinks/index.htm
The World Bank Gendernet links page, covering links to related websites maintained by the World Bank, UN, NGOs, etc.

Index

ABC of Gender Analysis (FAWE) 34, 108–13, 117–19
ActionAid 60, 66; *see also* Reflect programmes
Adolescent Peer Organized Network for Girls (APON), Bangladesh 50
Africa 6, 93, 97, 113; *see also* individual countries

Bangladesh Rural Advancement Committee (BRAC) 32, 41, 49–53, 131
Botswana 18
boys: abuse 142, 143; bias in the classroom 8, 112–13; in curriculum materials 112–13, 117, 121; drop-out rates 5, 62, 64, 65; educational opportunities 64; gender analysis 12, 18, 19, 35; *see also* participatory tools; Women's Empowerment Framework; masculinity issues 8, 10–12, 18, 19, 23, 138; peer group pressure 8, 10–12
Burkina Faso 5

Caribbean region 5
Changing Images (Obura) 34, 106–8, 113, 119, 121, 122
community involvement: *see* participation
Costa Rica 5
cultural factors: *see* social issues
curriculum 25
curriculum-materials analysis: action 109–10, 117–18; basic principles 102–13; boys' roles 112–13, 117, 121; classroom interaction 112–13; empowerment approach 60; formal education materials 34; gender identity issues 52, 102–4, 105, 107–8, 110–22, 123; gender relations examined 103, 106, 110; gender roles examined 103, 106–8, 109–10, 113–19, 120–2; girls' roles 112–13, 117, 120, 121; illustrations 112, 113–16, 121; language use 107–8, 110–11, 119, 120, 121; limitations 122–3; locus 110, 118; men's roles 103, 106–8, 113–18, 119, 120, 121–2; narration 109–11, 117–19; non-formal education materials 34; power 110, 119; qualitative analysis 34, 106, 107; quantitative analysis 34, 106–7; racial issues 118, 122; sources 34, 104–9; tools and checklists 34, 104; uses 122; visualisation 110, 118–19; women's roles 103, 105–8, 109, 113–19, 120–2

development agencies 4, 7, 9, 10, 127
development assistance: education issues 6, 14, 25; gender issues 6, 9, 10, 13–14; integrated approach 13, 14; Poverty Reduction Strategy Papers (PRSPs) 14, 25, 26; sector-wide approaches (SWAps) 14, 25; structural adjustment programmes (SAPs) 7, 26, 96
Dramaide, South Africa 138

158 | *Practising Gender Analysis in Education*

economic development: education relationship 2, 4–5, 7, 27; men's issues 2, 10; women's issues 2, 9–10, 11, 31–2, 36; *see also* development assistance

education: access 26, 58, 62, 64, 65, 68; achievement 8, 11–12, 26, 64; basic 24; conscientisation issues 50, 58, 61, 62, 63, 64, 65; control issues 44, 45, 52–3, 62, 63, 65; with development assistance 6, 14, 25; economic development relationship 2, 4–5, 7, 27; educational concepts 23–7; educational opportunities 4, 13–15, 50, 58, 62, 64, 104; *see also* Education for All; Universal Primary Education; formal 23, 42, 88–9; gender analysis 13–15, 17, 18–19, 21, 22–3, 30; *see also* Gender Analysis Matrix; Harvard Framework; Social Relations Approach; Women's Empowerment Framework; gender equality 13–15, 21, 45, 46, 52–3, 56, 92; government policies 2, 4, 5, 7; indicators 26–7, 61; informal 23–4, 42; in institutional analysis 88–9, 90, 91–2, 94, 95–7, 100; non-formal 23, 32, 49–51, 52–3; participatory approach 58, 62, 63, 65, 67–8, 81; *see also* participatory tools; resources 26, 44, 45, 52–3, 54; retention 9, 26, 27, 62, 64, 65; social issues 27, 86, 88; supply and demand 25; welfare equality 58, 63, 65; *see also* primary education; schools and schooling

empowerment defined 21–22

Education for All 5–9, 13, 24–5

Framework for Action, Dakar (2000) 2, 25

Gambia 5

gender defined 16

gender analysis: choosing tools 29–35; communication 31; data collection 13, 20, 39, 47, 54, 64, 84; defined 19; in education 13–15, 17, 18–19, 21, 22–3, 30; efficiency approach 9–10, 11, 31–2; empowerment approach 9, 10, 11, 12, 31, 32–4; gender budgets 23; gender concepts 16–23, 30; gender identity 12; gender needs 20–21, 30; gender relations 10, 17, 33; gender roles 9, 17–19, 30, 34, 68–9; men analysed 12, 17, 18–19, 20, 34–5; monitoring and evaluation 29, 31, 69, 72; participatory approach 3, 33, 34; *see also* participatory tools; as a planning tool 31, 54, 69, 72; purpose 2, 3, 4–9, 14–15, 19, 29–31; training 14, 54, 63; uses 29, 30–1; *see also* Gender Analysis Matrix; Harvard Framework; Social Relations Approach; Women's Empowerment Framework

Gender Analysis Matrix (GAM): background 71; basic principles 71–4; categories of analysis 73–4, 78, 83; cultural factors 33, 74, 78, 82, 83; data collection 84; in education 75–83; efficiency approach 32, 33; empowerment approach 33; gender needs examined 81; gender relations examined 71, 74, 80; gender roles examined 71, 81, 83, 131; gender sensitivity 72; levels of analysis 72–3, 78; limitations 80, 84–5; men analysed 35, 71, 72, 78, 81, 84; as a monitoring tool 64, 72, 75, 77–8, 80, 81, 83; as a participatory tool 72, 81, 84, 85; questions to ask 74, 77; uses 84

Gender and Development (GAD) approach 9–10, 11

gender mainstreaming 2, 11, 12–13, 40, 47

Gender Sensitive Editing (ADEA) 105, 120

Gender Sensitivity: A Training Manual (UNESCO) 34, 105–6, 119, 121–2

Ghana 18, 33, 60, 66–9

girls: abuse, *see* sexual harassment below; bias in the classroom 8, 112–13; in curriculum materials 112–13, 117, 120, 121; drop-out rates 5, 6, 9, 26, 62, 65; educational opportunities 5–7, 50, 58, 64, 104; female identity issues 10, 11, 12, 104; gender analysis 18, 19; *see also* participatory tools; Social Relations

Index | 159

Approach; Women's Empowerment Framework; HIV infection 93; peer group pressure 10–11; sexual harassment 44, 46, 95, 96, 99, 142–7 Global Campaign for Education 14 Governments: education policies 2, 4, 5, 7; gender budgets 23; gender policies 2, 6, 7, 20, 22, 23, 97; schools programmes 37, 41, 50, 52–3

Harvard Framework: access and control profiles 36, 38, 44, 45, 50–1, 52–3, 54; action plans 46, 48; activity profiles 36, 37, 39, 40, 41–3; advantages 51; background 36; basic principles 36–40; in communication 54; data collection 39, 47, 54; in education 40–51, 52–3; efficiency approach 9–10, 32, 36, 54; gender identity examined 50; gender needs examined 35, 39, 49, 64; gender relations examined 46, 47, 49, 5; gender roles examined 36, 37, 41–3, 47, 50, 64; influencing factors 36, 38, 39; limitations 54; men analysed 35, 37, 41–3; as a participatory tool 45, 50, 51, 55; project cycle analysis 36, 39; uses 54
HIV/AIDS 6, 33, 92–9, 129, 138

India 59, 76–80, 117
Indonesia 5
International Monetary Fund (IMF) 14, 26

Kenya 106, 130

Lesotho 5
literacy programmes 33, 66–9, 80–3, 129–30, 135

Malawi 22, 32, 80–3, 113–16
men: benefits measured 44, 46, 53; community work 43; in curriculum material 103, 106–8, 113–18, 119, 120, 121–2; in economic development 2, 10; empowerment issues 2, 21, 33; gender analysis 12, 17, 18–19, 20, 34–5; *see also* Gender Analysis Matrix; Harvard Framework; participatory tools; Social Relations Approach; Women's Empowerment Framework; marginalisation 2, 6, 9, 10, 30, 34; masculinity issues 10, 12; resource access 38, 44, 45, 52; *see also* boys
Millennium Development Goals 2, 25
Mozambique 5

Namibia 5
Nigeria 32, 39, 41–8, 51, 54
Non Formal Education Programme (NFPE), Bangladesh 32, 41, 49

Oxfam 4, 14, 33, 60

Participation: defined 33, 58, 125; in education 58, 62, 63, 65, 67–8, 81; for empowerment 125; in gender analysis 3, 33, 34; limitations 3–4, 126, 127–8, 137, 148; by women 50, 58, 63, 65, 67–8, 81, 148; *see also* participatory tools
Participatory Learning and Action (PLA) 124
Participatory Rural Appraisal (PRA) 1, 3, 34, 124, 125, 127; *see also* participatory tools
participatory tools: 'abuse' spiders 143, 144; action plans 132, 141; activity profiles 135–6; boys analysed 130–1, 138, 142, 143–4; calendars 130–1; defined 33, 34; in educational context 126, 129, 130–1, 132, 135–7, 138–40, 142–7; in gender analysis 64, 124, 127; gender relations examined 130, 138, 139, 143–4, 146; gender roles examined 129, 130, 133–4, 135–6, 138; girls analysed 130–1, 138, 142–7; limitations 33, 126–8, 137, 148; maps 129–30, 142–3; men analysed 130; pie charts 135; problem trees 132, 143–5; problem walls 146–7; role play 137–8, 146; solution circles 147; sources 124–5; SWOT analysis 132–3; time lines 138–9; trees 131–2, 143–5;

160 | *Practising Gender Analysis in Education*

uses 34, 148; Venn diagrams 133–5;
see also Gender Analysis Matrix;
Harvard Framework
Participatory Workshops (Chambers) 124–5
Philippines 5
primary education: availability 2, 4–5, 24, 25; gender equality 5, 6; retention 5, 6, 26
Primary Education Project, Tanzania 14, 19, 33, 60–5, 83

racial issues 11, 45, 91, 92, 118, 122, 126
Reflect Mother Manual (ActionAid) 125, 129, 139, 140
Reflect programmes (ActionAid) 33, 60, 66–9, 80–3, 124
resources: in education 26, 44, 45, 52–3, 54; institutional responsibility 91; men's access 38, 44, 45, 52; women's access 36, 38–9, 40, 44, 45, 52–3, 54

schools and schooling: bias in the classroom 8, 112–13; curriculum 25; *see also* curriculum-materials analysis; enrolment 26–7; HIV/AIDS prevention programmes 33, 92, 93–9, 129; peer group pressures 8, 10–12; school fees 7, 26, 89, 96; sexual harassment 44, 46, 95, 96, 99, 142–7; social issues 8, 11–12, 25, 27, 86; *see also* education; primary education
Senegal 92
sex-disaggregated data 13, 20, 39, 47, 64
sexual stereotyping 8, 17, 22, 40, 111, 121
silk reeling project, India 76–80
social issues: in education 27, 86, 88; gender equality 7, 9, 16–18, 20–1, 95; in schools 8, 11–12, 25, 27, 86; social capital 27; social relations 17, 47; *see also* Social Relations Approach; for women 7, 17, 33, 47, 74, 78
Social Relations Approach (Kabeer): background 86; basic principles 87–92; in education 92–9, 100; empowerment approach 33; gender identity examined 87, 94, 95, 97; gender needs examined 91, 96, 97, 98, 99; gender relations examined 33, 46, 94, 98, 99, 100; gender roles examined 91, 92, 95, 96; gender sensitivity 97, 98, 99; girls analysed 95, 96, 99; institutional analysis 33, 86, 88–92, 94, 95–7, 100; limitations 86, 100–1; rules 90, 91, 92; social relations 33, 87–8, 90–1, 95; strengths 100; uses 100
South Africa 5, 138
South America 5
Sri Lanka 5

Tanzania 14, 19, 33, 60–5, 83, 130, 136
teacher training college, Nigerian 32, 39, 41–8, 51, 54
Textbooks as an Agent of Change (Brickhill *et al.*) 105, 119–20
Thailand 5
truancy 5, 9, 12, 62, 64, 65

Uganda 33, 92–3, 94–7, 98
UN Girls' Education Initiative (UNGEI) 14
Universal Primary Education (UPE) 2, 4–5, 25

Welfare Approach 11
women: access equality 21, 58, 59, 63, 65; benefits measured 38, 44, 45, 46, 53; community work 19, 30, 34, 37, 43, 109; control equality 58–9, 63, 65, 68; in curriculum material 103, 105–8, 109, 113–19, 120–2; in economic development 2, 9–10, 11, 31–2, 36; economic issues 7, 18, 47, 52, 53; educational opportunities 5–9; empowerment issues 9–10, 11, 12, 21, 31, 32–4, 56; *see also* Women's Empowerment Framework; participation issues 50, 58, 63, 65, 67–8, 81, 148; productive work 9, 18, 30, 34, 37, 109; reproductive work 18–19, 30, 34, 37, 109; resource access 36, 38–9, 40, 44, 45, 52–3, 54; sexual harassment 96, 97; in small businesses 75–7, 81, 108; social issues

Index | 161

7, 17, 33, 47, 74, 78; 'triple role' 19, 30, 34, 37; welfare equality 11, 58, 59, 63, 67, 68; *see also* girls
Women in Development (WID) approach 9, 10, 11
Women's Empowerment Framework (Longwe): background 56; basic principles 56–60; boys analysed 64, 65; in education 50, 51, 58, 59, 60–9; empowerment approach 10, 33, 51, 69; gender needs examined 21, 35, 59, 62–5, 81; gender relations 70; gender roles examined 58, 59, 62, 64, 65; gender sensitivity 50, 58, 62, 63, 65; girls analysed 62, 64, 65; levels of equality 57–9, 63; levels of recognition 59–60, 63, 65; limitations 69–70; men analysed 35, 56, 64; uses 69
workshops 3, 34, 124, 128–9, 142–7
World Bank 10, 13, 14, 26
World Declaration on Education for All, Thailand (1990) 5–6, 24–5
World Education Forum, Dakar (2000) 2, 5, 25

Zambia 5